A CUP OF COMFORT®

for D🐾g Lovers

Stories that celebrate
love, loyalty, and
companionship

Edited by Colleen Sell

Adamsmedia

Avon, Massachusetts

For Brianna, my little dog lover,
whose doggie dreams will one day come true.

Published by
Adams Media, an F+W Publications Company
57 Littlefield Street, Avon, MA 02322. U.S.A.
www.adamsmedia.com and *www.cupofcomfort.com*

ISBN 10: 1-59869-269-0
ISBN 13: 978-1-59869-269-3

Printed in the United States of America.

J I H G F E D C B A

Library of Congress Cataloging-in-Publication Data
A cup of comfort for dog lovers / edited by Colleen Sell.
p.   cm.
ISBN-13: 978-1-59869-269-3 (pbk.)
ISBN-10: 1-59869-269-0 (pbk.)
1. Dogs—Anecdotes. 2. Dog owners—Anecdotes.
3. Human-animal relationships—Anecdotes. I. Sell, Colleen.
SF426.2.C85 2007
636.7—dc22   2007017702

This publication is designed to provide accurate and authoritative information with regard to the subject matter covered. It is sold with the
understanding that the publisher is not engaged in rendering legal,
accounting, or other professional advice. If legal advice or other expert
assistance is required, the services of a competent professional person
should be sought.

—From a *Declaration of Principles* jointly adopted by
a Committee of the American Bar Association and
a Committee of Publishers and Associations

Many of the designations used by manufacturers and sellers to distin-
guish their products are claimed as trademarks. Where those designations appear in this book and Adams Media was aware of a trademark
claim, the designations have been printed with initial capital letters.

This book is available at quantity discounts for bulk purchases.
For information, please call 1-800-289-0963.

Contents

Acknowledgments

My heartfelt thanks go to:

The authors whose stories grace these pages and to the 2,500 or so other writers whose stories I thoroughly enjoyed but could not publish in this book;

You, dear readers, for allowing us to share these stories with you;

The stellar team at Adams Media, particularly Meredith O'Hayre, Laura Daly, Paula Munier, Gary Krebs, Beth Gissinger, Tracie Telling Barzdukas, and Jennifer Oliveira.

My husband, Nikk, for supporting me in my work, for being my light and my laughter, and for bringing Woody into my life.

Introduction

"He is your friend, your partner, your defender, your dog. You are his life, his love, and his leader. He will be yours, faithful and true, to the last beat of his heart. You owe it to him to be worthy of such devotion."

Unknown

Upon turning eighteen recently, my eldest grandson used his birthday money to buy two items that, as a minor, he'd been forbidden: a tattoo and a dog. The tattoo surprised me. Scott, an honor student and athlete, doesn't strike me as the tattoo type (whatever that is). The dog, though, had been a long time coming. Scott has longed for a dog since he was a toddler. From the age of five, he even knew which dog he wanted: a Siberian husky. Only a husky would do . . . until his 18th birthday, when he met, fell for, and bought an English bulldog. That surprised me a little too. Nash's price tag flat-out floored me. The pup cost more than my daughter's (Scott's mom's) first car!

Nash was worth every cent. Scott adores him, and so does Scott's adorable girlfriend, Amanda. Scott's mother, Jennifer, on the other hand, was not so enamored. A drooling, loose-skinned, slack-jawed, sixty-pound puppy is an acquired taste, even for some dog lovers. Jennifer is not a dog lover.

Then one day, Nash plopped down next to Jen on the sofa, singling her out from the other six people in the room, including Scott and his crazy-for-dogs, ten-year-old sister, Brianna. Heaving a big love sigh, Nash then rested his head on Jen's knee, where it remained for the rest of the movie. A few days later, he rested his big slobbery jaw on Jen's shoulder as she was driving.

"That was it," Jen told me later, "I was a goner. Couldn't help it. He's so sweet."

I wasn't quite the pushover. Though I loved dogs as a young child, I became fearful of them after a stray German shepherd attacked me while I played in our backyard. Our tiny terrier mix, Tally, came to my defense before the shepherd could seriously hurt me. Tally jumped up, sunk her teeth into the big dog's neck, and wouldn't let go. I ran into the house for help. When my mom, armed with a shovel, and I reached Tally, she was lying on the grass, bleeding, and the shepherd was gone. The stray apparently had distemper, and Tally succumbed to it several weeks later. I was heartbroken, but from then on, I was leery of dogs.

As the mother of three kids and the wife of a "dog person" who felt that kids and dogs go hand-in-paw, I welcomed . . . well, allowed . . . several dogs into our family. But I didn't really love them.

When my kids were all grown and gone, I relished the freedom of being pet-less. No fish. No birds. No lizards. No dogs. Then I fell in love with, you guessed it, a dog lover. When we met, Nikk was dog-less, still mourning the loss of his beloved pit bull, Baron (short for The Red Baron, after the *Peanuts* character Woodstock's alter ego). Apparently, our romance helped heal his heart, because before long he wanted another dog.

I protested: "Look, I'm just not a dog person."

"Well, I am," he insisted. "He'll be an outside dog," he said. "I'll train him and take care of him," he promised. "All you'll have to do is love him." He grinned.

"Don't hold your breath," I said.

Not long after, Nikk came home with a six-week-old border collie/Australian shepherd mix—with a beautiful, silky coat and the most intelligent and expressive eyes I've ever seen in an animal. Nikk considered naming him Linus, another Peanuts character. (Before Baron, there'd been Snoopy.) But to honor me, the writer, he named our new pup Woodstock ("Woody"), after the character who typed his masterpieces atop Snoopy's doghouse.

True to his word, as he always is, Nikk took full responsibility for Woody's care and trained him to be an obedient, quiet farm dog. He comes inside the house only if invited—when the weather is bad or when he's under the weather. Even then, he has to be coaxed, and he always stays in the laundry room—without being commanded to "stay." He is quite the gentleman.

Very smart. Extremely athletic. Highly skilled. Affectionate. Devoted.

Goodness, I'm bragging about my dog. Yes, *my* dog. Somewhere along the way, Woody became mine, too, and true to his breed, guarding me became his most important "job." For nine years, he has been my walking buddy and fierce protector. To think of life without him brings tears to my eyes, so I push those thoughts aside and think, instead, of all the "Woody stories" that brighten our days.

I used to wonder how dog lovers could sit around talking about their pets the way other people tell stories about their kids and grandkids and the good old days. Having truly loved a dog, I no longer wonder. Oh, the stories I could tell about my Woody!

How he jumped a ten-foot fence to reach me after I'd done a face plant while hoeing my vegetable garden, a no-dog zone he'd never before breached. I woke up to Woody licking my ear, nudging my arm with his paw, and whining pitifully.

How he chased away a big brown bear that had rumbled across our path during a walk.

How he wailed outside my bedroom window as I wailed on my bed inside, the day I received the devastating news of my son's neurobiological disorder and the grim prognosis it entailed. The sound of his sympathetic howls snapped me out of my keening and made me smile.

He makes me smile often and enriches my life in countless ways. I've got so many Woody stories to tell, I could fill a whole book with them.

But this book isn't about my dog. *A Cup of Comfort® for Dog Lovers* is filled with heartwarming stories about the canine companions of other dog lovers. I hope you'll enjoy these stories as much as I enjoy my dog, Woodstock.

~Colleen Sell

Bloodlines and Heartstrings

There's no denying the beauty of purebred dogs—the perfection of lines, the even coloring, the uniformity of features. Lovely. I also strongly believe in obedience training, whether that consists of formal classes or extensive home training, to teach pets social manners and to make them easier to live with. It's a tenet of good pet ownership. But sometimes bloodlines and training take a backseat to good, old, scruffy mongrel love. Such is the case with our much-adored pound puppy, Frinkle.

Frinkle? Um, yeah. The name conjures up images of a prissy toy poodle or a yapping bichon frise, doesn't it? However, Stinky Frinky, as I like to call her in criticism of the perfumes she rolls in, is our huge-as-a-bear rottweiler-cross. Maybe it will help if I explain she was named by our four-year-old son, Liam, who has Asperger's syndrome.

Liam is our special child, in the same way Frinky is special. Sometimes it takes the eyes of love to see unusual value. Asperger's, like other forms of autism, reduces a child's ability to relate to others. Though his Asperger's is fairly mild, it was enough to make him incredibly lonely and isolated as a young child, which is why we'd decided to visit the pound for some permanent pet therapy. Who says money can't buy love?

"A small dog," I insisted, as we wandered through the cages of forlorn canine faces. "Something my son can handle and nurse in his lap."

Liam and his dad nodded and stared at the over-full cages of unwanted beasts. I'm sure if Liam had been allowed, he would've taken all the dogs home. They looked like they needed someone to care. Then he laid eyes on Frinkle and stopped walking. With a soft yip, she galloped over to stick her velvety muzzle through the bars, her tail wagging in circles so quickly it was a wonder she didn't take off. Liam's eyes grew as round as two full moons.

"I want this one," he yelled, stroking her floppy ears and being licked like the world's last lollypop.

I glanced at the Godzilla-sized paws, the broad head that spoke of her rottweiler blood, and the wonky back leg that looked suspiciously like an expensive vet-care-requiring hip dysplasia.

"Honey, you want a small dog that will fit in your lap," I reiterated.

"She's small," he argued.

Compared to what? Mount Everest? Okay, so the puppy would fit in his lap at the moment, but she was barely eight weeks old. Anyone could see this creature would shoot up faster than Jack's magic beans and be fe-fi-fo-fumming around my kitchen in no time. I'd be the no-gold goose for agreeing to this purchase, and we'd have to extend our mortgage to feed her. Besides, didn't rottweilers have a bad reputation for turning on their owners? I think they were once used for hunting bears. That's not what the mother of a young child wants roaming freely with her unpredictable offspring.

I firmed my lip and shook my head no. End of discussion, right? Um, no. That was logic talking. Try explaining those reasons to any four-year-old, much less one with Asperger's. The inevitable happened. My son squatted by the cage to hug Frinkle through the bars. She whimpered in an I-was-made-for-you puppy voice. I stared at the two lovers locked in their fast embrace and caved faster than a spelunker. It likely saved us all time, effort, and tears, anyway, because Liam was determined not to look at any other dog and would have worn me down eventually. Love never gives up, the Bible says. So true. Especially when it's driven by a preschooler's tenacity.

From the moment we brought the over-pawed puppy home, she was my son's dog. She followed him around, sniffing his heels, stealing any sandwiches he waved too low, and resting her brown eyes on him with such adoration that we expected her to melt into a large chocolate pool at his small, dirty feet. Anywhere he went, she followed. Anything he did, so would she. It was like rearing conjoined twins. Never did I see the slightest sign of aggression from her. She had to be the sweetest-natured dog on God's green earth.

But despite her dedication to Liam and hours of frustrated lessons from both of us, her leash technique left much to be desired—*much*. Like Pooh Bear's Tigger, Frinky loves to bounce. Leash, no leash, it's all the same to her. When you weigh as much as she does, one bounce does the trick. Everything attached to you bounces too, and keeps bouncing like a series of seismic shocks. Taking her for a walk is hazardous to dentures. Even half an hour after her spaying operation, the vet couldn't stop her from almost leaping out of her stitches in the recovery cage. He said he'd never seen a dog do that before.

Then he saw Liam bouncing with excitement

to see his dog when we came to pick her up. He smiled at me and said, "She's his, isn't she?" No denying that, no matter whose name was on the ownership papers.

So where do purebred dogs come into this story, you ask? Well, one day when Frinky was about three years old, my son read in the newspaper that a new vet surgery center was setting up in our area, and as part of their opening celebration they were having a "top dog" competition, open to all hounds in the community.

Liam tapped his finger on the ad as he slurped his glass of milk at the kitchen table. "I'm going to enter Frinkle," he said confidently.

I almost choked on my tea. I squinted at our shaggy mutt and her clumsy disproportioned body. Though she ate everything not nailed down and was the size of a small airliner, she never quite grew into her paws. Sure, we loved her, but form? Grace? Style? Those were mere words in the dictionary and not appropriate here. The tutu-wearing hippos of *Fantasia* sprang to mind. Frinky noticed me looking and wagged her tail. It thumped the floor. China rattled in the cupboards.

Liam's eyes were bright. He didn't have a doubt in his body. "She's sure to win," he said with an enormous grin.

Oh, brother! I looked at Frinkle again. Win? Only

if she ate the competition. I tried my best, but nothing would dissuade or distract Liam from his purpose.

The day came. There we stood, holding the end of a lead with a huge bouncing dog on the other end. We tried to wend our way through the crowds of beautifully coifed, pure-bred, perfectly behaved beasts. Outclassed? You bet. The noses around me might have been cool and wet and stuck up in the air, but mine was red hot and wrinkled with embarrassment as I tried to whistle and pretend I wasn't being dragged up to the registration desk by a canine yo-yo. If I could have sunken into the grass I would have.

"We want to enter my dog, Frinkle," Liam said as soon as his turn came to talk to the woman jotting down entrants.

"Sorry," the sweet-smiling receptionist said into his eager face, "but only adults can enter the dogs."

"Oh." His face fell. My heart twisted. Frinkle spun her head to look at me, goad me, shame me into giving her a chance. So I did. I signed her up. I figured I was already so embarrassed at the leap-and-drag display through the crowd that having her run amok in the obstacle course couldn't make it any worse.

We took our position as part of the crowd at the side of the track and stood watching a series of stunning dogs. They jumped through hoops, walked across beams, and slithered under tarps. No way would Frinky do any of that. She'd never even seen half of this equipment before, much less done an obstacle course. The only thing I knew she'd excel at was eating the bowl of dog food they were promoting. They'd be lucky if she left the placemat it rested on.

Our turn came. The judge called our name. The people around us parted. I was Moses, and my face was the Red Sea—or should that be a sea of red? Oi. My heart pulsed in my neck. I stepped forward. Why had I agreed to this? Humiliation has never been my thing. I would probably insult these pedigree pooches and their owners just by being there. I wanted to turn tail and run. Only my lack of a tail and the look of absolute confidence on my son's face kept me from following my base instincts.

Then I had a brain wave. I edged up to the judge and whispered in his ear, while Frinky bounced excitedly beside me and nearly jarred my arm off.

"This is my son's dog, and I know that, for insurance purposes, you need an adult to show her, but would you object to him being involved by running with her?"

The judge looked at my unruly dog, then at my hyperactive boy, then at me. His face crinkled with compassion. "Guess so," he said with a smile. "This is supposed to be a family day, after all."

I breathed a sigh of relief and walked back to

the starting line. I patted my son on the back and brought him forward with me. "Did you see what the other dogs did?" I asked him.

He nodded vigorously.

"Think you can do the same?"

More nodding.

The starting horn hooted. Liam was off, legs chugging as fast as I'd ever seen him run. I released Frinky's leash. She bounded after Liam, shadowing his every move. Where he climbed, she followed. Where he wriggled, so did she. When they got to the food dish, she needed no demonstration. She sucked up the mound of special dog food in a single gulp. The crowd went silent. I think they were in shock. When Frinky and my son came galloping over the finish line in record time, having not missed a single obstacle in the course, a collective cheer went up! Frinky leapt for joy! Her boy leapt too! Me? I was too teary and choked up to say anything. When it came time to accept Frinky's trophy, Liam didn't hesitate to step forward and to say thank you. My throat was constricted with emotion.

In the car on the way home, Liam and Frinky cuddled up and looked at their trophy. I swear that dog was smiling. Of course, it might have been because she was anticipating the huge bag of promotional dog food that she'd won as a prize.

Some nine years later, I'm happy to say that both dog and boy are doing well. Liam has quite a few friends these days, having learned ways of working with his challenges. But none of his friends could ever replace the puppy who loved him through the hard years, the dog who would follow him to the end of the earth and who did for love what breeding and teaching never could.

~Lyndell King

Sisters

I don't know if Mom instinctively chose a puppy that was like her, or if the puppy chose her for the same reasons, or if it was all a coincidence. What I do know is that the tiny mixed-breed puppy Mom named Simba looked much like a lion cub, with reddish-gold fur and a black face, and had pride and personality to match. She was a formidable lady, benevolent but alpha, exactly like my rock of a mother.

My family had moved from a Massachusetts suburb to the wild Vermont countryside, settling on a long-defunct farm complete with old wooden wagons and spiked metal tines hidden in tall field grasses, a decaying barn full of mysteries, and woods full of once lively logging trails. There were endless opportunities to run and explore. I stayed outside for hours on end, my mother knowing I was in good hands with Simba.

Although we found Simba at a shelter, there was no question in her mind that she was a queen, and at four years old, I was already clear who was the wiser of the two of us. There was something almost magical to me about the dog's confidence, and I can recall thinking of her as an older sister. By the time I was five and she was just over a year old, I was following her about and learning valuable lessons under her guidance. I trusted her wisdom, because no one had taught me not to. No one had said, "She's only a dog." No one filled my head with ideas of animals being any less than me or of animals lacking intelligence and running through life as near robots, functioning on rude instinct alone. I saw only the wise sister's confident dog grin and Simba looking back at me to make sure I wasn't lost. I knew if she told me something, it was true.

Dogs can't speak like we can, but I understood what Simba communicated to me. She put her nose to the ground and moved with purpose, telling me there was an interesting animal ahead and I must be quiet. Sometimes it was a woodchuck we'd spy in a field. Other times she'd lead me to partridges and flush them, leaving eggs by a tree base to investigate. Once, Simba inadvertently led me to a skunk, and by the way she had barked from a distance, I knew it wasn't anything I wanted to be close to. By watching her and learning from her, I became a crafty hunter in my own right, observing and approaching snakes, frogs, and birds with stealth until I could grab them with as quick a move as Simba's snapping jaws. I'd let my prey go after looking at it a while, though, while Simba sometimes killed hers. That was the one point we didn't agree on. Still, whenever I caught something, she'd sit back and look at me with a wide dog smile and squinted eyes, as if I'd learned my lesson well and she was satisfied. I lived for that look.

She gave me sharp stares if I did something she wanted me to stop, and she refused to go where there was danger. On the second winter at the farm, snow pelted our rural north country and built up in record levels. It was days before I could look out and see more than a few feet ahead of me, but when the sun finally came out again, the world was a wondrous vanilla-milkshake-coated land. Simba said this stuff was marvelous to play in, and she asked me outside by jumping and snapping at the snow and then play-bowing before me with a mischievous twinkle in her eyes. Since I always listened to Simba's good ideas, my human sister, Karin, and I raced out together. Bundled against the cold, holding sleds, and laughing wildly, we plummeted down fresh drifts as Simba ran alongside, grabbing our boots and pulling them off. It made me furious, in a way, when I was left with stocking feet in the snow while Simba raced away, tail waving and thoroughly pleased with her catch, but I never thought of punishing her. She held rank, after all.

Later, after retrieving our boots, Karin and I decided to spend some time exploring the barn. There seemed to always be a new discovery in there—stalls and mangers where horses once fed, bits of metal that had unknown purposes, leather straps, piles of hay, dark corners and places you feared to walk because the boards creaked and groaned even under small feet. We had explored the barn many times, with Simba leading the way and telling us where we should step and where we shouldn't. Mom always said, "If Simba won't go there, then don't go." Simba wisely picked the best paths and enjoyed the forays as much as we did, even though she had to be the responsible one at all times.

This snowy day was different. With Karin and I encrusted with balls of ice and with Simba's leg feathers similarly encumbered, we approached the barn doors only to have Simba erupt in a flurry of angry barking. We stopped dead in our tracks and turned to see Simba facing the doors, hackles raised and practically frothing at the mouth with fury. When we moved to open the door, Simba snarled and snapped at the door, and we both stepped back from whatever was agitating her so.

Our parents were on the house roof, shoveling snow piled at least two feet deep. "There must be an animal or something in there!" Our mother called down to us, "Stay out!" She didn't have to say another word. We knew better than to disobey both Mom's and Simba's directives.

The moment we turned from the barn doors, Simba stopped barking, but she continued to pace and to behave like she was worried. I didn't know what awful creature could be inside the barn, but I knew it was nothing I cared to face. I wondered aloud whether there were mountain lions here.

"Maybe it's a rabid raccoon," my father suggested.

Karin and I carefully climbed the ladder to be closer to our parents on the roof of the house. The only sound was their shovels *phloofing* into the snow, scraping along shingles, and then the snow floating and landing almost silently on a growing pile in front of the house.

The view was incredible, and I'd almost forgotten about Simba pacing at the foot of the ladder when a thundering crack pierced the air and then rumbled, vibrating through my chest. Our heads snapped up just as the sound faded, and we watched in awe as the roof of the barn collapsed, the sound proceeding the fall, caving in almost slow motion, with some of the walls following, until what was once a majestic old building was nothing but a crumpled heap of old lumber and a milk house standing alone.

No one said a word for the longest time—at least, that's how I remember it. None of us had any idea the barn would collapse, but Simba had known. If we hadn't listened to what she told us, Karin and I would have been inside at the very moment the beams gave out, with no chance of getting out in time. I can't recall what we did for Simba that night, but I'm sure we recognized her good deed. You see, my parents were never the kind of people who thought animals were less than we are. Simba was part of our family. She was my wise sister, and I'm thankful with my very life that I didn't grow up with the notion that she was anything else.

~Tanya Sousa

A Gift Returned

Don't worry, Mom. You'll never have to do a thing for this dog."

Those were the exact words that came out of my fourteen-year-old son's mouth as he toted his twenty-four-pound Dalmatian puppy down the hall. Bringing the pup home that evening marked the culmination of years of Jamie's begging and writing letters to me, pleading for a dog. I had always resisted, as I was never much of a dog person, and I was also a young widow raising two sons. The last thing I needed was a dog, but I finally gave in one Christmas and presented Jamie with a three-month-old spotted puppy, which he himself had chosen and named Chaz. As my son carried his furry gift to his room that first night, he vowed he would take full responsibility for the new member of our family.

For several months, Jamie *did* take very good

care of his Christmas present, proudly taking his dog on walks around the neighborhood and making sure he always had food and fresh water. He was elated to return home from school each afternoon, giving his new buddy a big hug upon entering our house. I frequently picked Jamie up from school, and I would occasionally take Chaz with me. As Jamie approached the car, he and Chaz would break into two very different grins at the sight of one another.

Initially, I felt pretty good about the gift I had bestowed upon my elder son. During those critical early months of training, however, the dog had some "accidents" in the house, causing me to question whether I had made a huge mistake. Seemingly overnight, my clean, dander-free home was transformed into a kennel of sorts, with the faint whiff of canine chow emanating from the laundry room and a fine coating of white hair glazing my hardwood floors. The dog was cute, but he certainly hadn't won my heart . . . completely. Thankfully, Jamie crated his pup, trained him to take care of his needs outdoors, and showered him with loving hugs. My duties were limited to paying for the food and veterinary expenses.

As school and sports began to require more of Jamie's time, he spent less and less time with his dog. Like most Dalmatians, Chaz would get into things if he didn't have his daily walk, so I started taking him for afternoon jaunts. I had always been a solitary walker, and the companionship of the growing creature proved a bit of a challenge for me. I discovered that squirrels and rabbits were highly desired objects, and I can't count the times I had to let go of the leash and chase the dog through the neighborhood.

Being a dog owner was no fun for me, and after paying a few thousand dollars for a fence and an obedience trainer, I was certain that buying the dog had been a major mistake. My son was happy with his dog, but he was no longer living up to his promise of taking care of him. I, however, was quite miserable. I had spent some serious dollars on Chaz, and my home had turned into a petting zoo, with a dog, two cats, and a ferret. Was I crazy?

I considered giving the dog away. I knew Jamie's heart would be broken, but he had not kept his word. Chaz was lucky if he received an occasional pat from his master, and I was frustrated, dreading the years of living with the dog. When talking with friends, I heard myself uttering the words "that stupid dog" on an increasingly frequent basis. Something had to change.

As I sat on my screened porch pondering the situation one morning, I arose to let Chaz inside. Not paying attention, I accidentally shut the door on his tail, resulting in a loud yelp from the victim, whose chopped tail splattered blood on the carpet and all over the walls of my foyer, dining room, and hall. An hour later, he was in surgery, having part of his tail removed. As I paced the floor of the veterinarian's clinic, guilt flooded me. This dog had constantly shown me affection, but I had resisted it, and now I had inadvertently lopped off his tail. When I thought about the joy he had brought to both my sons and the ways he happily bounced around when he saw me, something in my heart changed.

That incident sparked a turning point. Over the next couple of months, Chaz and I began to bond rather well. I cuddled with him a lot and took him to the veterinarian twice a week to soak his tail. Due to continued infection, we decided to have the tail amputated. Every time our tail-less, brown-eyed pooch looked helplessly at me, I realized I was becoming quite enamored with him. At the same time, I became less frustrated with Jamie for relinquishing his duties. I started to fall in love with the spotted bundle of playfulness.

Shortly after the tail catastrophe, Chaz began sleeping at the foot of my bed. Our daily walks became more enjoyable for me, and I was always happy to return home in the afternoons to see that smiling face at the dining room window, eagerly awaiting my entrance. He was becoming for me a welcomed friend and family member, and he was gradually becoming my dog.

During my son's high school years, his dog and I continued to grow closer. At various times, Jamie took him for runs in the neighborhood and would give him a pat on the head, but that was the extent of his involvement. I knew he recognized I was becoming the dog's master when he presented me with a photograph of Chaz in a heart-shaped frame that reads "My One and Only."

When Jamie went to college ten hours from home, he apparently missed his dog a lot. He'd e-mail me a few times a week, always adding, "Give Chaz my love." Upon arriving home for the winter holidays, the young army cadet would gleefully give his four-legged friend a huge hug, rolling around with him and reminding the family that this pet was the best gift he'd ever received. One evening as Chaz, Jamie, and I sat on the sofa, I asked Jamie if he planned to take his dog when he graduated from college. My son looked me in the eyes and said, "Mom, I could never do that to you. I love Chaz, but he's really your dog now."

Jamie is now a married military officer who has another dog. He rarely asks about Chaz these days, but I'm certain he has a special place in his heart for this animal that he wanted so badly many years ago. It was a gift I reluctantly gave to him, and the gift has been returned to me. His dog is now my constant companion, who runs to me when he's frightened, licks my face when I'm having an occasional cry, and frequently places his head on my shoulder in the middle of the night. It's difficult to think of life without him, yet I know pets are placed in our lives for only a limited time. In our years together, Chaz has given me the gifts of learning to find the joys in each day and of attempting to practice unconditional love.

I sometimes think about that chilly December evening when Jamie chose Chaz from among his canine siblings. He could have opted for any of them, but Jamie told me there was just something special about the rather hyper one. I now say a daily silent prayer of thanks for the slightly overweight vessel of unconditional love that has made such a difference in the life of this single mother.

In stepping back on his promise to take care of his Christmas present, my son ultimately returned his gift to me—and my life has forever changed.

~Amy Walton

Converting Ray

"Want to pet Lucky?" I asked, smiling up at my new boyfriend, Ray, as I stroked my neighbor's Australian shepherd. "She's so soft."

"I'm not a dog person," Ray said matter-of-factly.

Bad news. The man of my dreams absolutely loves dogs. But Ray had such a terrific smile.

Ray and I quickly found that we shared many interests: biking, hiking, ballroom dancing. He was gentle and sweet with his adult children and mine. Within weeks, we were spending all our free time together. When Ray tolerated my yellow Lab, Isabelle's, frequent goosing the moment he came in the door and included her in our walks and hikes without objection, I decided that he was a dog person after all. He just didn't know it. Yet.

The day that I had to put Isabelle down because of an aggressive lung tumor, Ray held me as I cried.

I knew in his heart he must be grieving too. We were talking of marriage by then and planning to buy a house together. I broached the subject of a new dog.

"Let's talk about it later," he said.

Out of respect for my loss of Isabelle, he waited several months before reminding me that he'd clearly said he didn't care much for dogs.

"You know, honey, you actually are a dog person," I said. "Look how much you enjoyed Isabelle."

"She was part of the package. And sure, she was a lot of fun. But now we're going to have a new home. Dogs track in a lot of dirt. They get hair all over."

"You could go running with a dog."

"I can also go running without a dog. Sorry, babe. I just don't get jazzed about looking into their eyes and carrying on whole conversations with them like you do."

Dogs do track in a lot of dirt. Most breeds do get hair all over. And I had never seen Ray look into Isabelle's eyes. Because Ray was by far the best of the men I'd dated in the ten years following my divorce, I would try living without a dog.

I tried for six months, devoting myself to planning our wedding and house shopping. I had plenty to keep me busy: caterers to call, invitations to address, wedding cakes to sample. Still, I felt a physical ache when Ray and I were walking or hiking and passed someone with a dog. I wanted to please Ray, but I needed a canine buddy.

I mailed the invitations, and we hired the minister. We found a house and began packing our respective things. The ache deepened.

A month before the wedding, I subscribed to a community newspaper where ads for dogs free to good homes frequently appear. I fully intended to read only the local news until at least after the wedding. My rebellious fingers opened to the classifieds. I scanned the ads, and felt mostly relief when nothing jumped out at me. For several weeks, just reading those ads pacified me. Then, Annie, a golden retriever, jumped off the page.

"You know how desperately I miss having a dog," I told Ray. "I've tried living without one, but I just can't resist going to see this golden retriever. Please, will you go with me?"

"Isn't our wedding in two weeks?" he asked.

"I know the timing's lousy. I won't get her unless she's absolutely perfect. If she is perfect, I'm sure my friend Lynn will keep her while we're on our honeymoon. We've traded dog sitting before."

"I thought you wanted new carpet for the house. We could never keep it clean," he said gently, his expression clearly pleading, "Be reasonable."

I couldn't be reasonable. "I need a dog," I said,

my voice breaking and tears smarting my eyes. "I wish I didn't, but I do."

"Go see her then," he said with a tone of resignation.

As I drove to see Annie, part of me hoped she wasn't perfect. I didn't want to add stresses to a new marriage. Another part of me danced.

Eighteen months old, her coat as red and rich as a chestnut mare's, professionally trained so that she heeled like a champion show dog, just the right height to pat without bending over as we walked, Annie was perfect. She came complete with a crate and a tracking chip in her shoulder.

"She's awfully big," Ray said when I brought her home.

Big dog, big mess, I knew he was thinking.

"I'll vacuum every day," I promised.

"We'll see," he said.

That night, Annie and I had an eye-to-sad-brown-eye, nose-to-slightly-damp-nose talk. "Annie," I told her, "Ray is a dog person, but he doesn't know it. And he has to find out, or we're both in trouble. Your job is to convert him."

Annie thumped her tail twice on the hardwood floor. "Sure. Of course," she seemed to say.

Annie stayed with Lynn while Ray and I honeymooned, and then she moved into our new house with us. She began her assignment immediately.

"I'm going jogging," Ray said and sat on the steps of our front porch to tie his running shoes.

Annie followed him out the door and stood beside him, leaning ever so slightly against his shoulder.

He looked at her. "You want to come?" he asked.

She opened her mouth in a big doggie smile and wagged her tail.

"Get your leash," he said.

I quickly got the leash and tied a plastic bag to it.

"Plastic bag?" Ray asked. Then, "Right. Gross, but a good idea."

"I love you both," I said, patting Annie and kissing Ray. I watched them jog down the street and then turned to my mountain of unpacked boxes.

An hour later, they were back. Ray plopped down on the couch. "She isn't very fast," he said. "But then, neither am I. The company's nice." He reached out and stroked her head.

You're making progress, Annie, I thought to myself.

Over the next month, Ray and Annie jogged several times a week. Ray had his heart set on the Portland Marathon, now that he was finally retired and had time to train. Annie had her heart set on joining him for every run. I watched them leave the house, both alight with anticipation. When they came home, I would give Annie a fresh bowl of water and Ray a beer.

In the house, Annie flopped her big body down in whatever room I occupied. In my Prius, she sat on a throne of two large, fleece-covered foam pads that allowed her to look out the windows as she accompanied me on all my errands. But when Ray went for his running shoes, she raced to the front door, then back to Ray, then to the door. I waved them off, glad to be second in her heart for a moment.

Just when they had this joyful routine down, both Annie and Ray started to limp. So I took them both to orthopedists. Turns out they had bad knees in common.

"Looks like we'll be walking instead of running," Ray said to Annie. This wasn't the first time I'd seen him chatting with her when he didn't know I was around. Then he turned to me, the lines of his face long with disappointment that he couldn't run the marathon, and said, "I guess Annie's a good dog for an old guy like me."

"I'm sorry for you both, sweetie," I said and kissed his forehead. Annie lifted her nose from her paws, looked at us, and thumped her tail in agreement.

Summer arrived with its host of pollen-related

allergies. Ray talked about the impact of dog hair on hay fever. Talked about it every single day. *Just when Annie and I were making such progress,* I thought. I vacuumed more in one month than I had in my entire life. We ran the furnace fan night and day and installed an air purifier in the bedroom. Ray felt a little better.

Meanwhile, Annie was having allergy problems of her own. She developed a hot spot on one of her front legs and chewed it raw no matter what we put on it. She never complained, never whined, never begged for extra attention; she just settled into the misery of worrying her hot spot when we weren't distracting her.

I took her to the vet, who gave her medication for her leg and flea allergies and put an Elizabethan collar—an affair that looks like an upside-down lampshade—around her neck. When we got home, we walked to the overstuffed chair where Ray sat reading the paper so Annie could model her latest fashion.

"Poor girl," Ray said, putting down the newspaper and reaching out to stroke her back. "That looks awfully uncomfortable. I could never wear it." He eyed her a few more seconds. "I thought dogs always whine when they're miserable," he said to Annie. "But you never do. I seem to be the dog around here." He smiled his crooked smile, and my heart swelled with love for them both.

With Ray and Annie's allergies under control, we all three set out one warm, sunny afternoon for a stroll around the nearby community college campus. When we were side by side, Annie walked closely at my left heel, unless I told her to run off and enjoy some doggie smells. If Ray or I walked a little ahead of each other, she created a place for herself between us, looking worriedly from one to the other. "You are both all right, aren't you?" her look seemed to say. "All three of us must stick together no matter what." No distraction kept her away for long.

Then Ray and I decided to go different directions. He wanted to head up through the buildings and find a restroom. I wanted to walk through the woods at the edge of campus.

"See you in a minute," he said, kissed me quickly, and headed off to the right.

I walked left toward the woods. Annie started off with me, but her head swiveled repeatedly to watch Ray's retreat.

I stopped and knelt down to talk with her. "It's okay. Go with Ray," I said.

I swear she understood. She looked at the spot where he was just disappearing into the complex of buildings.

"It's okay," I said again. "Go on."

Annie bounded after Ray. In a few minutes they were back.

"She wanted to go with me," Ray said, his voice holding the wonder of a small boy who has just been chosen for the team.

"I saw that," I said.

Ray knelt down and looked in Annie's eyes. His hands stroked her nose. "You know, girl," he said, "I didn't want to fall in love with you."

My grin must have been spreading clear across my face when he looked up at me and said, "Don't think this means I'm a dog person."

~Samantha Ducloux Waltz

Free Willy

I fell in love at the mall. Not with Manolo Blahniks or the latest fashion trend, but with a living, breathing being. On that breezy Sunday in April, I stood transfixed in the parking lot, looking at him, watching him. The world seemed to disappear as I gazed into his dark brown eyes, held him in my arms, and brought his face close to mine in a fit of unforeseen boldness. His nose felt cold against my skin. He seemed a bit frightened, even reluctant to pursue a relationship. But I was hooked, and I couldn't let him go.

So I handed a check to the breeder who had traveled several hundred miles to meet me in the mall's parking lot, and I took my new West Highland terrier puppy home.

My husband named him Willy, apropos of his willful nature. Once Willy got comfortable with his human pack and familiar with the new surroundings, he wasted no time in testing the limits. He would pull the leash in one direction while I yanked in another. Gnawed corners appeared on throw pillows, and a sandal disappeared. I decided it was time to nip this in the bud and enrolled him in puppy kindergarten. Besides, I wanted to show him off. He was so cute and smart; I predicted he would surprise the instructors and surpass their expectations. He would make Lassie look like an amateur. He would learn to save damsels in distress at the snap of a finger and perform tricks that would make an acrobat weep. I imagined agents clamoring to represent him, his paw print on Hollywood contracts, and requests for dog food commercials.

The first night of puppy kindergarten, Willy was ready and freshly groomed, his white fur radiant. He already knew the sit, shake (right and left), and lay down commands, tricks I'd taught him to make sure he would be a step ahead of the other puppies. While the owners introduced themselves and their pets at the start of class, I checked out the competition. There were other cute puppies in the class, a few even cuter than Willy. Oh well, if he couldn't be the cutest, at least he would be the smartest. Even beauty contests are based as much on how one answers questions as on physical beauty. We would have to rely on Willy's intellect.

At the end of the first session, our instructor handed out the upcoming assignment with the warning that if we neglected to work on these commands with our puppy during the week, everyone would know. I smiled to myself. Despite the late hour, Willy and I would start on the homework immediately. No playtime. No belly tickling. We would get down to business. It would be cold nose to the grindstone.

Upon our arrival home I got Willy ready for our training session and then searched in vain for the homework sheet. An hour later, it hit me. After class I had placed the homework on top of the car while getting Willy settled in his crate and driven off with the papers still on top. I called the training center, leaving a late night, frantic message on their answering machine. The next afternoon I heard back from the training center; they would leave another copy at their facility, which I could pick up at any time. For me, "any time" meant right now. Dinner with friends would have to wait. This was important. Willy could not lag behind. There was no way I was going to let other puppies, particularly the very cute Josie or Libby, surpass him.

I drove back, exceeding the speed limit, and with papers in hand raced back to our friends' home, gulped down dinner, made some polite conversation, sped home, and got a sleepy Willy out of his crate.

I then looked at the homework. It consisted of teaching your puppy to sit and lie down by the next session. Gee, he already knew that stuff.

The next seven weeks were agony . . . for me, not Willy. He was having fun; I was miserable. At home he performed the commands flawlessly. In class the word "sit" became a foreign language. He could not stay still, desiring instead to play with the other puppies or jumping on me to get to the treats in my pocket.

"I knew someone else whose puppy failed kindergarten," Libby's "mom" whispered as I pushed down on Willy's hindquarters to make him sit. Color drained from my face upon hearing the words. Could that be true? Would Whisper, Shannon, and Lance go to the next level while Willy did a repeat? Would my puppy be forced to wear the scarlet letter of shame? The thought of it was unbearable. So we worked harder. Again, at home he was perfection. In school I became the stranger he ignored.

Graduation day found me full of dread and with a stomach made for Maalox. Willy spent the hours before class calmly munching on his food and scooting after a butterfly or two. My friends informed me at the last minute that they couldn't attend the ceremony, perhaps due to embarrassment. Even my husband made excuses.

"Good luck, Willy," he called out as I was leaving. "Have fun tonight."

"I can't wait until this is over," I mumbled as Willy lurched forward, almost sending me headfirst into the screen door.

When we arrived, the seating gallery at the center was already filled. Cameras were at the ready, and videotapes were snapped in place by those who were there to record their pets' accomplishment. I looked down at Willy, and my eyes misted with tears. No one was there for him but me. No one to take a picture or applaud if he accomplished a sit-stay or ran through the tunnel. No one to smile from afar, turn to their neighbor, and proudly announce, "Do you see that little white Westie over there? That's Willy. He's so cute—and smart."

I wanted to comfort him, put my arms around him and tell him it would be okay. But he could not have cared less. For Willy, it was party time.

Willy did receive his diploma that night, despite doing a less-than-average performance on the obstacle course. I was proud of him as he trotted up alongside me, sat down, and watched as I was handed his diploma and some treats tied up with ribbon. After we got home, he chased after a bunny in the backyard, came inside, and promptly fell asleep in his crate. The piece of paper hadn't changed him.

During the eight-week training program, there were nights when I returned from class exhausted and depressed that Willy was not meeting my expectations. On those occasions my husband would admonish me, "Just let him be a dog."

Maybe he's right, I thought now, as I watched Willy sleep contentedly after his big graduation day. We humans spend our lives cramming ourselves into society's corset, worrying more about fitting in than being ourselves and in the moment, rarely taking time for peace and play and what's most worthwhile. We grow up wearing ties and tight-fitting shoes, and we wait obediently in line or to speak to a human voice on the phone. Though we might complain about the confines, we persist in fencing in everything around us: our spouses, our children, and even our pets.

Yes, maybe it is time to free Willy from the shackles of expected behavior that we humans seem so hung up on. Maybe he needs, at least once in a while, to return to that happy-go-lucky puppy with the adoring dark brown eyes who knew no tricks at all and yet captured my heart the moment I saw him in the mall parking lot.

~*Lori M. Myers*

Comrades

May 25, 1970

Marine Sergeant David A. Lummis thrashed about on his hospital bed. Unpleasant thoughts pestered his mind: *This is wartime. Some of my buddies won't ever come back. I am one of the lucky ones. Some luck.* When his nurse came to check on him, he asked to sit up in his wheelchair, hoping it would chase away the nightmares. It didn't work.

Yes, he had made it back. During the three months since his return, there had been plenty of time to think—when his legs, what was left of them, didn't hurt too much. Today was his twenty-first birthday, but there wasn't much to celebrate. He refused to think about his future. Why bother? With two pitiful stumps for legs, it seemed nothing but grim.

He had asked Aunt Gertrude for only one gift,

which he wanted desperately. He hoped and prayed she could get it for him. Throughout his childhood, she had showered him with love and attention. She'd always given him what he wanted for his birthday. For this birthday, he'd asked her to bring Buddha home.

For the thousandth time, his mind wandered back to Dan Nang and his first meeting with that dog. Was it only six months ago? It hadn't taken long for him to get attached to the scroungy mutt. He was a corporal then. She was a scrawny bag of bones, a Basenji with a broken tail and a bald spot between her eyes, where she'd been burned by napalm. One day she padded up to him, begging for his C-rations. One glance, and he knew she had received more abuse than food . . . or love.

A parade of mice, hamsters, snakes, ducks, and rabbits—all the pets he had as a boy—trooped through his mind as he ran an affectionate hand across the bald spot of the mongrel and shuddered. Dogs were a delicacy in Asia; this starving animal had come to him for food. He dipped in and presented the last scoop to the little beggar. Her tail wagged deliriously when he offered her the empty can. She polished it clean with her tongue and sat down at his feet as if to say "Thanks, mister. That tasted good." Instant bonding.

As he headed back to his afternoon duties, the dog padded along beside him. A native villager, observing this, told him he could have the dog—which might or might not have belonged to him—for five American dollars and a can of C-rations. Sold. He named her Buddha because of her bald spot.

From then on Buddha accompanied him whenever he stood his lonely patrols on the Vietnamese hillside. One night, while they were carrying out their routine mission near An Phong, disaster struck. He didn't see the land mine. A call for emergency medical assistance went out. A fellow marine placed a tourniquet on his legs until he could be flown to nearby Chu Lai Base Hospital.

"This is a bad one," the messenger warned. "Come as fast as you can." The rescue pilot would be holding the delicate strand by which his life was hanging. The chopper swooped low and dropped to the ground. Later, David would be grateful for the buddy who had saved his life, and he would thank the Lord for the pilot who delivered him to the hospital in just seven minutes.

Once he regained consciousness in the hospital and his pain eased, David tried to piece things together. *Where was he when he'd stepped on the mine? He and Buddha had gone to . . . Buddha? Where was Buddha? What happened to his dog?*

Three months after the accident, he was transferred to Philadelphia Navy Hospital. At least now he was near his home. His family could drive over from New Jersey to visit him.

Recovery was slow. A few years earlier he had been honored as Collingwood High's greatest running back. A husky 175-pounder then, now he was a paltry eighty-six pounds and missing both legs from just above the knee. War is hell.

He missed Buddha. He worried incessantly about her welfare and wondered whether he'd ever see her again. He'd confided his fears to Aunt Gertrude and begged her to find his dog and bring her to Philadelphia for his birthday.

"I'll do my best," she'd said.

He'd taken her promise as assurance. Now he realized he had asked for a miracle and pinned his hopes on a foolish request. There was a good chance Buddha had died when the land mine exploded. If she had survived, how would Aunt Gertrude find her? If his aunt could find Buddha, who would risk flying into enemy territory to pick up a fifteen-pound mongrel? Buddha could have forgotten him, or found a new marine who loved dogs and was willing to share his C-rations. Maybe she'd become some villager's meal for a week. He grimaced, as much from his gruesome thoughts as from the physical pain wracking his body.

When Aunt Gertrude contacted President Richard Nixon for help, she was told no funds were available for such an undertaking. Still, David held on to his hope of seeing Buddha again—today, on his birthday.

You might as well forget that, he told himself. *Some things are beyond even Aunt Gertrude.* He leaned back in his wheelchair and tried to sleep. He awakened to the sound of strange voices in his room. He opened his eyes just as gentle hands set a scraggly little dog on his bed. The dog eyed him inquisitively and sniffed. A spark of recognition lighted her eyes. A stubby, broken tail began to twitch. Then she scrubbed David's face with her ecstatic kisses.

"I am so happy!" was all he could say.

Aunt Gertrude had set in motion a chain of events that resulted in David's emotional reunion with Buddha. She'd met with Lieutenant Colonel William Holberg, a Maryland legionnaire, and he'd contacted Department Adjutant Dan Burkhardt on behalf of David and his dog. The legionnaires had raised the funds to find Buddha and bring her home.

In due time, a marine platoon had entered An Phong and scooped up the dog, who had been cared for by David's buddies after his accident. Buddha had been flown to Baltimore on a commercial flight. When Buddha's quarantine ended, Burkhardt accompanied by several legionnaires, brought her to David's hospital room.

Joy at seeing his dog again overwhelmed David. Eventually, the excitement subsided, and he and Buddha were left alone. Before long, a coarse-haired little dog could be seen happily tugging at the wheelchair.

David Lummis faced a long road to recovery, but the medics said he would walk out of the hospital on artificial limbs by the end of the year. With Buddha encouraging him, David knew he would too.

~Hope Irvin Marston

A Leave from Absence

Sometimes a pet's name doesn't sink in—doesn't take. I read once that pets, especially dogs, can best learn their name if it contains two distinct syllables. Perhaps thus was spawned Fido and Fi-Fi. So when we tagged our animal-shelter survivor Cosmo Topper Puppy Moore, his moniker was doomed from the beginning. He learned the Puppy part, and the rest of his label seemed to fall on peanut-buttered ears. So Puppy it became.

Puppy was epileptic. We didn't know dogs could be, but yes, the recurring seizures are not unlike those of their human counterparts. But he lived beyond his odds, finally giving in to the toll at age fifteen. Owners all know that the loss of a pet exacts a predictable reaction.

"That's it," I said. "No more dogs. I never want

another. I can't go through that pain again." My wife, Kay's, bear hug signaled that she felt the same.

For eight years, we were satisfied with our lone housecat, Read-'em-a-Clipping News Carver Moore. Knowing that cats only answer to Kitty-Kitty—and only if they choose to—we deliberately splurged on his name.

One Saturday afternoon, at a large outdoor market near Dallas, we saw signs directing visitors to Pet Island. We thought, *A petting zoo? Let's check that out.* Instead, it was a pet marketplace, where vendors and breeders came together in a truer sort of "flea" market. It had a festival atmosphere, complete with clowns and characters dressed in stuffed-animal attire. There was Winnie the Pooh, Tigger, some sports-team mascots, and a couple of gigantic pullets flapping about, trying to take wing. I also recognized the celebrity Smokey Bear, apparently on fire-holiday thanks to recent rains. All these frolicking critters were handing out animal crackers to the children.

"It's just Disney-like hypnosis—a marketing gimmick for the kids out here," I muttered cynically.

We strolled past pens and containers with boas, miniature goats, and pot-bellied pigs—the "desperation" choices for pet lovers, or at least intended for folks more adventurous than me. Then I saw the picket fence, with an ivy-covered gate labeled

"Man's-Best-Friend Resort." My thoughts raced back to Puppy Moore, and I tarried at the entrance. Just out of sight, I could hear the joyful mingle of excited yelps and shrieks of joy from small children. It would be a mistake to enter here.

Kay touched my arm softly, beckoning me on with welled-up eyes. We moved through the gate together, as if facing up to some intentionally delayed appointment.

These were not common sale grounds. AKC professional kennels and regal-sounding breeder farms dotted both sides of a cedar-shavings walkway. It was a red-carpet welcome. No hawking of wares, no carnival hucksterism. Instead, it was a best-behavior collection of well-groomed and coiffed animals—with masters to match.

The Rocking-A Kennel caught my eye. Their breed line was the Australian shepherd. For me it was a first introduction. I had never met an Aussie. From the rack, I browsed their pamphlets about the coloration choices: blue and red merle. With faces less sharp than Lassie, the adults still showed strains of collie or maybe border collie, but with the odd ending of a bobbed tail. I was impressed with what appeared to be a perfect blend of strength and poise. I was also mystified by their eyes—one gold and one blue.

The parents of the litter were being presented to

the public in royalty fashion. They were sitting on a spread of artificial turf, almost engulfed by an amphitheatre of trophies and ribbons.

"Sire Tommy-On-Cudgegong and Dame Rachel Wurnshire-Heather," the sign said. *So much for simple two-syllable names*, I thought. Cosmo Topper Puppy Moore suddenly seemed more sensible.

Next to this pedigree-castle sat a child's playpen. Inside were the princes and princesses of the crown. As we leaned into the enclosure, our faces must have looked like Halloween lanterns beaming from above. As each of the four puppies stared up with cocked heads, one scrambled toward us from the farthest corner. He reared up on hind legs and strained toward my nose with all his power. As he got close, I swear I heard something of a whisper from him . . . "Pick me!" There. I heard it again. "Pick me," the voice said, this time with emphasis.

I plucked him from the playpen and held him to my chest. He was the size of a child's football, mostly fur, with a red tongue darting in and out. His whimper spoke louder than any car salesperson's wail. There was no putting him back. I paid the price without even haggling, waving away the checkbook demon that so rudely reminded me that my first house payment wasn't this much.

On the ride home, we agreed to call him Quigley,

after the character in the Australian-setting television show. From the beginning, he has validated the wisdom of our selection many times. I have marveled at his innate kindness and intelligence, his remarkable obedience, and his penchant for wanting to herd anything that moves, including the occasional errant dust bunny.

Raising pets, like rearing children, is the great educator. Profiting from experience, Kay and I had agreed on certain strict house-pet rules. Early on, it was evident that these rules were all unnecessary. Potty and furniture training were mastered so quickly that our home soon became free range.

We have learned that the more time we spend with Quigley, the more he is able to reveal his intelligence. We were struck by his ability to accurately identify each of his four rubber chew-toys. They are the same size and shape; they differ only in color.

"Get your red one," I say, showing off to friends.

"Now go find your black one." Works every time.

My friends all remind me that dogs are color blind. My Internet searches have all supported that notion. I don't claim to understand it. All I know is when I say, "Quigley, go get your yellow one," he does. So I just accept it as a wonderful gift and constantly search the pet stores for new colors to add to his palette.

I have never read a book about Aussies. I have learned about Quigley by observing and interacting. I can cup his face in my palms, lock his eyes with mine, and see far into his soul. I can sense in those moments he is returning the favor. In times of laughter his wag signals that he gets the joke. In distress or sorrow his nuzzle assures us he understands. If we leave the house without him, he welcomes us back with frenzied murmurs and frantic smooches. Competing for those special rushes of attention, my wife and I may be heard to whisper . . .

"Pick me."

~Lad Moore

Butkus on Guard

I was single, in my thirties, and had just purchased my first home. If I'd had a hat, I would have thrown it up in the air! It was a little lonely coming home to an empty house, though. To fill the void, I'd put on the television and watch the neighborhood kids playing outside from my kitchen window.

My favorite latchkey kid was Nick, an eight-year-old who had beautiful, sad brown eyes and a distinctive cowlick that made his sandy-brown hair dangle over his forehead. Nick always welcomed me home with a smart-alecky wisecrack that made me laugh.

One day, I saw Nick's older sister shove him and knock him onto his rear-end. She was the local bully, and everyone was afraid of her. Nick hit the pavement hard! When he got up, she went after him again.

I ran outside and broke up the brawl. Nick's elbows were bleeding, and his cheeks were bright red with embarrassment. His eyes were moist, but he mustered up every ounce of his eight years of manhood and refused to cry. I asked Nick for his mother's phone number.

"She won't be home until really late. Besides, she won't care, and Patty will only get madder. But thanks. I was afraid it was going to get bad. Patty's nuts," Nick said.

That incident forged a bond between Nick and me. From then on, though, when he greeted me with his trademark devilish grin and a wisecrack, I also saw the sadness in his eyes. Somehow, it made me feel even more lonely.

So when my best friend, Sandy, launched into her puppy sales pitch for the millionth time, I actually listened.

"Beth, you need a puppy to love and come home to."

"How can I have a dog? I work all day. It wouldn't be fair to a dog to be locked up all alone for hours at a time." I sighed.

"Have one of those kids come in after school to take care of the puppy for a few hours," she suggested. "Trust me, the kid and the puppy will love it, and you'll love it. I have a litter of Labradors, and one of them has your name on it!"

Sandy was right. One of them did have my name

on it, and I named him Butkus. He was an adorable, chubby black puppy, whose little pink tongue immediately attached itself to my face.

Butkus came with everything I needed, including a manual and a laundry basket, where he slept sweetly as I carried him to the van. He was so small, I hoped I could keep him alive. I'd never cared for anything living before. I felt like I was carting home the Hope diamond.

I soon discovered my "diamond" was less than flawless. We hadn't gone a few miles before the van filled with a horrible smell that made me gag and seemed to come from the back. The rancid odor was quickly accompanied by odd rustling noises, also coming from the back of the van. Suddenly, a cold wet nose poked me. Then the nose was gone! Again and again, Butkus poked his snout into the front seat and then disappeared, returning to whatever he was doing back there. *What did I get myself into?* I panicked. The smart thing would've been to pull over. But I was on a major turnpike where the shoulder was only for emergencies, and having a naughty puppy didn't qualify as an emergency.

I finally arrived home and practically fell out of my van, desperate to get out of the stench and to find the missing puppy. I opened the side door and stuck in my head. Butkus proudly showed me the remains of my instruction manual, remnants of it still hanging from his mouth. Terrific. Sandy was a dead woman.

I tossed Butkus into the basket and headed for my condo. Nick, as usual, appeared out of nowhere and attached himself to my hip immediately. He and his friends roared with laughter over the puppy in the basket. Nick shot off questions like a machine gun. Stressed, I was harsh with Nick. "Nick, I don't have time now. He's mine, and he pooped in my company van! I can't clean it up and watch him and talk to you all at the same time!"

Instantly, I regretted my outburst and tried to make up for it with a weak smile at Nick. Unscathed, he returned my smile. "I'll hold the puppy, but I ain't cleaning up no poop!" he said and busted out in a clown grin.

"Deal! Here's my key. Turn the laundry basket upside down over him, to trap him in it like a cage. And wait inside with him while I clean this up."

Nick scooped up Butkus as if he *were* the Hope diamond. Hugging the squirming puppy and beaming at his friends, Nick scurried inside.

From that day on, Nick had a strong bond with Butkus and spent every minute he could with him. At first, my mother pet-sat while I was at work, and she told me Nick would jump off the school bus and race directly to my door every day. He'd sit on the floor doing his homework until Butkus stole a vital piece of schoolwork. That would launch their game of Catch the Thief, with Nick chasing Butkus around the house as if he were in big trouble! My mother would sit on the couch enjoying the show.

Nick would stay all afternoon and be there when I arrived. My mother often asked whether Nick's mother might be wondering where he was. He would always deflect the question with his trademark wisecrack.

One day I arrived home to find Nick standing on a stool with Butkus in the sink. Butkus was covered in soap bubbles, and so were Nick and the condominium. My mother slept on the couch.

"What's going on, Nick?" I asked.

"Your mom left Butkus in his cage too long. He rolled in poop, so, I'm giving him a bath."

"So you do do poop, after all." I smiled, barely containing my smile.

Nick and Butkus were inseparable. The combination of the nine-year-old kid and the bigger kid with a tail became too much for my mom. Besides, she said, Nick could handle Butkus himself and didn't need her around anymore. But I was concerned about him being so young, so my neighbor agreed to greet Nick with the key and to keep an eye on things.

I went to Nick's house to ask his mother's permission to give her son an after-school job. I could hear yelling inside the house, but I knocked anyway. The apartment was filthy, and she came to the door reeking of stale booze. I couldn't help but wonder how bad Nick's life was. His mom said she "didn't care where he was." Her words would haunt me for years.

I made sure I always had healthy snacks, and some not-so-healthy, and a sandwich waiting for Nick at my home after school. He also took his money, but Butkus always had a new toy the next week. They continued to play Catch the Thief, which wasn't their only game, just Nick's favorite. Nick said he liked it because he could tell his teacher, "My dog ate my homework," and prove it, complete with bite marks. Butkus was always a willing participant!

Life rolled on, and when Butkus was about one year old, I married Chuck. We lived in the condo another year, before Chuck and I bought and moved into a new house across town. On moving day, Nick wasn't able to control his tears as he clutched Butkus's neck like a lifeline. My heart broke when Chuck gently separated Nick and Butkus, promising Nick he would bring Butkus back for weekend visits.

One Saturday Chuck came home earlier than usual. Butkus came into my room and put his wet nose on my face, waking me up. He wore his sad look on his face. I looked around to see what he'd chewed up.

"Nick's gone. None of the neighbors knows what happened or where he is. I'll try again next week," Chuck told me. "Beth, Butkus went nuts. It was awful. He ran around, looking everywhere. I had to drag him into the car."

Chuck went back three times. We never found out what happened to Nick.

Nine years passed, and I owned two dogs. When the doorbell rang or someone knocked on the door, it was pure doggie mayhem. So early one evening I greeted the pizza delivery guy outside. Syco, who is sly for a 150-pound dog, snuck out behind me anyway.

Standing before me was a tall, athletic, handsome, young man. He had light brown hair with a cowlick dangling over his forehead and twinkling brown eyes that seemed vaguely familiar. As I paid for the pizza, he looked at me curiously, too, while he petted Syco. Then he noticed a novelty stop sign that hung on the side of the garage. It had a picture of a black Labrador retriever and read "Butkus on Guard."

"I once had a dog named Butkus. Well, he wasn't really my dog; I just pretended he was. I dog-sat for him when I was a kid. He meant the world to me."

"Nick?" I asked in astonishment.

His head snapped up, and our eyes met in recognition. He tossed my pizza on the hood of his car and threw his arms around me in a bear hug. He stepped back and looked at Syco and then back at me, a sad question etched on his face.

"He's old, but he's inside," I assured him, smiling.

"Ah, man, you're kidding me! Do you know how many times as a kid I dreamed of seeing Butkus again? This is unreal! Do you think he'll remember me?"

"It's been a long time, and you're all grown up now—and handsome, I might add! Butkus hasn't changed, though; he'll love you whether or not he remembers you," I said. "If he does remember you, he'll sing. That's what he does with my sister; he sees her only once every few years, and he loves her like crazy. We call it his 'crazy love song.'"

I opened the front door. The instant Butkus spotted Nick, he began his serenade—a combination of a high-pitched howl and a bark that he holds like a bad opera singer. Snout in the air, Butkus sang and sang. Nick dropped to the floor and threw his arms around Butkus, muffling "my buddy" into his neck repeatedly.

When Nick came up for air, there were tears in his eyes. He said that coming home to care for

Butkus had been the only thing in his life then that had meant anything. If he hadn't had that, he really didn't think he would be here today. Every day, he recalled, he'd practice telling what was going on at home by confiding in Butkus, his best friend. One day he looked into Butkus's eyes and swore he felt Butkus tell him something back—that it was time to tell for real. So he promised Butkus that he would. Whenever Chuck brought Butkus back for those weekend visits, Nick would feel guilty that he hadn't told yet. So he finally did.

"Social Services took me away from that whole mess. And yeah, it sucked at first. But my aunt and uncle stepped up, and they've been great. I work for my uncle now, and I'm paying my way through college."

Nick looked at me with those brown eyes of his, now filled with sincerity rather than sadness, and said, "Thank you, Beth." Then he petted Butkus, smiled, and said, "And thank you, Butkus. You certainly were on guard."

After Nick left—with a big tip and an invitation to visit anytime—I shared my pizza with Butkus. Although the pizza was cold, my heart was warm.

~*Beth Rothstein Ambler*

A Heeling Heart

There was little discussion of who would keep Tag, my brother's young, black Labrador retriever, after John's death. Tag was a living connection to John, and though a grief greater than my own was unfathomable, I knew my mother needed Tag most. She had lost her broad-shouldered, broad-grinned son. She needed Tag, if only to curl up with, when death's demons haunted.

Tag and my mother mourned together. During their first year, a solid rap on the door would enervate Tag into a full-body wagging enthusiasm he had reserved for his master's return. In the seconds before rationality reigned, Mom, too, would hope my brother was about to bound into the house. She had hung John's Carhartt jacket and ratty baseball cap on a hook above his cowboy boots in her mudroom. It deluded her that he would be coming back from Colorado for Christmas vacation, with another semester of veterinary school under his belt, on the days when denial was her only method of survival.

John and I had often booked the same flight from Denver to Chicago to descend on Mom in unison for the holidays. On this winter morning I sat alone, squeezed between strangers. I dreaded Christmas without John. Uncovering the ornament he had made in first grade or his knit stocking, stretched out from our tradition of flooding each other with gag gifts, reignited anguish that felt new and raw all over again. At least I had Tag to look forward to. I couldn't wait to see that dog.

I was approaching our prearranged meeting place outside O'Hare airport when I saw them—the unmistakable combination of my stylish mother behind the wheel and a slobbering, yet regal, Tag, straining out the back seat window. My mom and I greeted each other cautiously, not out of animosity, but restraint. We innately knew that if we held each other's gaze, the sorrow of another holiday without John would overwhelm our weak levy.

"I'll sit in back with Tag," I said in a desperate attempt to throw sandbags between our grief. "How's my boy?" I asked into his eyes while ruffling his ears and scratching him under the collar, where he liked it best. As we pulled away from the airport, Tag straddled my lap to resume his position at the window. Breathing his freshly shampooed scent, I rested my head on his side and hid my burning eyes from Mom's glances in the rear-view mirror.

Despite the lapses between visits to my mother's house, Tag and I were inseparable when we were under the same roof. He slept at the foot of my bed, trotted down the stairs after my slippered feet, waited as I fixed my coffee, and even joined me in the bathroom as I showered and blew my hair dry. What made this unusual was that Tag was generally aloof. While my mom adored her dog, she complained that he wasn't cuddly, that he'd always give her his rump to scratch instead of his muzzle. I couldn't help remembering that John was the same way. As the only male in our household for many years, John would often put the brakes on touchy-feely stuff. He told my mom he would give her backrubs—he on the couch, she sitting in front of him on the floor—only if she refrained from pleasurable noises. An "ooh, that feels good," and his hands were in the air. "I'm outta here," he would say and be off the couch, heading to the kitchen to pour himself a Coke.

My practical self attributed Tag's uncharacteristic affection to my resemblance to John. We're both fair-skinned with honey-colored hair, possibly even sharing a common smell or pheromone. But my spiritual self believed it was more than that—that part of John's soul was with Tag and when Tag and I were together, John and I were too in some way.

In fact, until this trip home for the holidays, I had sometimes wondered if I should have inherited Tag. Tag's adjustment would have been less jarring if he had stayed with me in Colorado and had an owner who was closer to John's age and lifestyle. Yet, I knew my motivations were primarily selfish, and now I was witnessing how beautifully Mom and Tag were piecing their lives together.

Mom had resumed her work as a photographer, and Tag now chased water birds along the shores of Lake Michigan rather than the chickens John kept on his property near the Rocky Mountains. Tag now heeled alongside Mom, though to her right side, the way my left-handed brother had purposely trained him, so that he'd be away from the rifle on their occasional hunting trips. Tag's stellar behavior evoked a pride in Mom, not only of Tag but also of her son's fine ability with animals. Mom glimpsed John through Tag the way one sees a deceased loved one in a child who bears their likeness.

As Mom and I sipped coffee in front of the Christmas tree on my first morning home, she invited me to witness a pet-assisted therapy program that she and Tag had become involved with over the last year. In phone conversations, Mom had mentioned the program in passing, but it wasn't until now that I'd had a chance to really talk with her about it.

She told me it had started when a stranger remarked how well trained Tag was.

"Yes, he is wonderful, but that credit really goes to my son," Mom had explained.

During the brief conversation that followed, the stranger said he volunteered with a group that helped others through the use of dogs. Then and there, Mom had resolved to sign up.

The next day, however, she'd questioned whether she had the emotional strength to work with people who had disabilities. We were grateful John's departure from this world had been quick and peaceful. His girlfriend had smiled between sobs as she recounted that she and my brother had been goofing off on the mountain just moments before John, an expert skier, had inexplicably collided with a tree, rupturing his aorta. John had at least not suffered debilitating injuries—unlike many of the people whom my mother would train Tag to assist.

Despite her hesitations, Mom summoned the courage to contact the organization. "My name is Mary Ann Alexander, and I have my son's dog. Well, he is my dog now," she began.

The compassionate voice interrupted. "I know

about your son, Mary Ann. My husband works with John's father. I was at the funeral. My name is Carole Hunt." This was an almost eerie coincidence in a city the size of Chicago. My mother's resolve to train Tag in pet-assisted therapy was restored. Tag was hers for a reason. Maybe this was it.

When Mom received the pet therapy brochure in the mail a few days later, she settled on the rug beside Tag to read it. The literature emphasized that, more than providing companionship, these therapy dogs helped with the rehabilitation of patients. The dogs needed to be not only well trained, but also gentle enough to work with children and vibrant enough to engage a person whose spirits or energy may be low. Therapy dogs must also be patient and unbothered by wheelchairs, walkers, back braces, or helmets, as well as the awkward movements and vocalizations of some patients. Few dogs pass the rigorous obedience screening on the first try. The test date was only two weeks away.

"You'll do it, Tag," Mom said, as she slid onto her side to lock eyes with her best friend. In a rare but increasingly frequent show of affection, Tag covered her face with kisses.

When the time came, Tag obeyed every instruction with an attentiveness that would have made John proud. Tag and my mother were invited into the program.

Now, sitting in Mom's kitchen a year later, I saw no trace of the initial butterflies she'd had as she saddled Tag with his official work vest in preparation for tonight's session. I, however, was nervous, even in my limited role as an observer. Then I remembered Mom commenting that Tag's omniscient look had allayed her fears. When I saw the purpose in Tag's eyes, I knew I'd be all right. In that moment, my internal compass needle, haywire for over a year, regained its bearings.

Tag looked handsome, even cocky, as he leaped into the back seat to be driven to the Rehabilitation Institute of Chicago (RIC). From the front seat I turned to tell him, "You know John wants you to do this, don't you, smart boy?"

Mom's eyes smiled—the sandbags between us long gone—as we pulled onto Lakeshore Drive. The elevator door opened to a large recreation room milling with patients, therapy dogs, and the dogs' owners. Mom's preeminence in the program showed as she was swallowed by the group to answer last-minute questions before the therapy began. Eventually, all dogs and volunteers, paired with their patients, were spread throughout the room. In one corner a young man negotiated trading his walker for a leash, while a teenage girl pressed her dormant vocal cords to command a dog to sit.

For Mom and Tag, this was the last night of a

six-week partnership with a seven-year-old girl named Samantha. In an automobile accident on Christmas Eve, Samantha had lost her little sister, and she had become partially paralyzed on her right side. She was in a wheelchair and had lost much of her speech. An older sister and both parents, who had survived the wreck with minor injuries, were there to cheer Sam on.

Sam had fallen in love with Tag the first night they worked together. Initially, Sam would pet Tag only with her left hand, until my mother, remembering her training, urged Sam to pet him with her right hand. As Sam fought to communicate with her right side, Tag nudged her hand with his wet nose. It was the magic touch. Sam giggled, evoking a gasp from her mother, who hadn't heard her laugh since before the accident. Slowly, Sam's hand obeyed her brain's signal. She extended her clenched fist enough to knock on Tag's shoulder. It was a tremendous achievement.

Every Tuesday night for six weeks, Tag helped Sam overcome her paralysis. Sam learned to uncurl her fist to accept a tennis ball and then to throw it to Tag, who retrieved it and begged for more. Their favorite game was to balance a dog biscuit on Tag's nose while he waited for the command to nod his head and catch the biscuit. Now Sam's actions with Tag were almost fluid, and she said his name clearly.

Sam's mother, Julie, told us that every time they got into the car, the little girl would ask, "Tag?"—hoping they were on their way to the RIC. I listened as my mother shared with Julie her story of losing her son. My mother hadn't wanted to burden Julie with our loss. Tonight, though, as Julie presented my mother with a bouquet of flowers for all she had done, it seemed appropriate. Upon hearing about John, Julie commented, "Your son was going to be a veterinarian so he could heal animals, but now his animal heals people."

With Christmas behind me, I boarded my flight back to Denver. As I buckled my seat belt, I noticed Tag's straight, black hairs covering my beige corduroys and smiled. Brushing the hair from my lap, I thought about how Tag was with me in more ways than just his shedding coat. Tag had taught me, my mother, and even Sam's mom, Julie, that there is hope after tragedy.

In the days after John's death I had fearfully asked Mom, "Will we ever be okay again?" She responded that she didn't know how we ever could be. Yet, we *are* okay—due in large part to a huge-hearted black Lab with a wise old soul.

~Emily Alexander Strong

Green Roof, Red Car, Dog on Roof

All dogs are individuals. Most have an endearing trait or two. Some have one unique habit that the whole neighborhood knows—and talks—about.

As a puppy, Ina, a standard schnauzer, was like most other puppies: active, cheerful, and curious. She loved to watch things that happened around her.

Two days after our family brought our new puppy home, my neighbor knocked on my door. He asked, "Do you know your dog is on the roof?"

We have a two-story house with the front door on the ground level and the main living quarters on the second level. A bay window in the living room overlooks a small overhanging roof that extends half the width of the house and then joins with the garage roof.

Of course, I didn't know my dog was on the roof.

I ran outside, looked up, and sure enough, there on the roof was my seven-week-old puppy.

I ran back inside, up the stairs, into the living room, and to the open bay window. I leaned out to look at my puppy—who, alternately, looked up at me inside the house and down to my neighbor who was standing on the ground watching both of us.

I called and cajoled and coaxed Ina to come back inside, all the while contemplating whether I was going to have to climb out onto the roof to get her. Ina moved very slowly and hesitantly toward me, an inch at a time—not out of fear, but because she didn't want to come back inside. When she was finally within arm's reach, I stretched as far as possible without falling out the window myself, grabbed her by the scruff, and pulled her safely inside. (My next purchase would be a collar.) Satisfied that my dog was safe, my neighbor went home.

A few days later, another knock sounded at my front door. My neighbor was back.

He pointed upward. "Do you know your dog is on the roof again?"

This time I didn't step outside to look. I ran straight upstairs and again tried to coax the dog to come where I could reach her. However, this time she wasn't as willing to be dragged inside. It took a little more time, but I did get my puppy back into the house safely.

The next day, as I walked from the kitchen into the living room, I just happened to look in the direction of the bay window, just in time to see the little tail and bottom of a naughty white schnauzer disappear out the window.

I stood in shock and called her name.

Ina hopped back inside, wagged her stubby tail, sat, and looked at me, pleased with herself for obeying.

I closed the window anyway.

But we don't have air conditioning, and it's hot in August. The next day, the window was again opened, and again the dog jumped outside. This time, however, she jumped back inside on her own. She played in the house for a few hours, but it wasn't long before she jumped back outside. She paced back and forth on the roof, and then sat at the eave for the rest of the day, quietly watching the cars and people go by. Though she appeared to have no intention of jumping, I still didn't think it was a great idea for her to be on the roof. Though it wasn't steep, it was angled.

The next day, I ordered screens.

The day after that, the screen for the bay window had a schnauzer-sized hole in it, and the dog had upped the stakes. She was no longer content with the ordinary roof. This time she scaled the garage roof and was sitting on the peak.

I gave up.

So instead of watching my dog on the roof, I watched people watching my dog on the roof.

I live in a quiet, suburban, uneventful residential neighborhood. Or at least it was uneventful, before Ina came to live with us. Now people walking by stopped and pointed. Some gasped, while others laughed.

Cars stopped in the middle of the street, and people strained, some leaning out their car windows, to watch the dog, now positioned like a gargoyle at the peak of the garage, her paws hanging over the edge, head on her paws, her prominent schnauzer nose protruding past the edge for everyone to see. Sometimes, people even got out of the cars to stare. Fortunately, we don't get a lot of traffic on our street.

Many times, I heard people talking as they walked, staring in wonder, asking each other whether the gargoyle on our roof was real. Then Ina would move, answering their question. When the gargoyle moved, most people jumped. One elderly lady screamed.

It didn't take long before strangers began to knock on my door to ask the same question as my neighbor: "Do you know your dog is on your roof?"

I assured them I did know, thanked them politely, and sent them on their way. But after the first two or three curious visitors, Ina decided she didn't want people touching her house.

Being on the roof gives one a distinct height advantage. When a new person approached the house, Ina ran to where the person had to walk beneath the roof to get to the front door. She leaned down on her haunches and told them, loudly and in no uncertain terms, what she thought of a stranger coming too close to her house.

A full-grown standard schnauzer weighs between forty-five and fifty pounds. As Ina grew into adulthood, her rooftop ruckus grew less cute and more threatening as, the bigger she became, the further down she could lean. She also became more confident and expanded her limits accordingly. Several times she leaned down over the eave so far that I don't know how she never fell. This brought her bared teeth not so very far above anyone brave enough to walk beneath them.

Of course, having a dog patrolling the roof of one's house isn't totally a bad thing. The sight of flashing fangs and pearly white teeth accompanied by the resonance of sharp barking above people's heads sent most door-to-door salespeople to our poor neighbor's house. We didn't need a security system.

We had our own live burglar alarm right there on the roof for all to see, in snarling glory. She didn't bark at our friends (or our neighbor); when they came to the door, she would run back and forth on the roof, silent, her tail wagging. We knew who was approaching the house by our dog's actions.

When we took Ina for a walk, strangers would stop us and ask, "Is that the dog from the roof?"

After giving directions to our house over the phone, people would pause and ask, "Is that the house with the dog on the roof?"

Before long the directions to anyone who lived in the area were simply "green roof, red car, dog on roof." The inevitable response was, "Oh, I know your house."

Then one day when Ina was barking, indicating an unknown visitor, I did what I always did. Before going downstairs, I looked outside to see if I recognized the car. It wasn't a car. It was a van. The SPCA van. A man wearing a green uniform was standing in the middle of my driveway, looking up on the roof at my barking dog. I knew I was in trouble.

Even though I reasoned it was probably too late, I tried to call Ina in. It only made her worse. She alternated between running back and forth on the roof and leaning over the eave to bark and snarl.

When the man dared to walk beneath where Ina

hovered above him and go to the door, she jumped back inside the bay window, bounded past me, and ran downstairs to the door to "greet" our visitor.

Since he'd already seen her, I didn't bother locking Ina up. Holding her firmly by the collar, I opened the door.

The man didn't smile. He bluntly informed me that someone had complained, saying that I was locking my dog out on the roof.

I explained how Ina's trips onto the roof were completely voluntary as well as how we had tried repeatedly to stop her, but couldn't. After I reminded the gentleman of what he had witnessed, he reluctantly agreed that the dog did enjoy being out on the roof. He also acknowledged that, with the window open, she was free to go in and out as she pleased. Once assured that the dog was healthy and happy and not in danger, he turned to leave.

The second the door closed, Ina dashed up the stairs, bounded through the living room, jumped out onto the roof, and ran straight up to the peak of the garage to watch, no doubt pleased to see the last of the SPCA officer. With Ina once again in her familiar gargoyle position, I stood at the window, also watching him leave.

But he didn't leave. Halfway to his van, he turned around and started to come back. Ina scuttled down and positioned herself above the doorway. The man stopped and looked up at my darling dog, lips curled, teeth bared, poised and ready, and daring him to walk beneath her, so she could once again voice her opinion.

He looked up at me and asked the question that makes many dog owners cringe. "Does your dog have a license?"

"Yes, my dog has a license."

And, yes, I know my dog is on the roof of my house.

She likes it there.

~Gail Sattler

Puzzle

 W hat's this?" Ed asked, holding up the envelope.

"Fan mail," I replied, trying not to sound smug.

"You got a fan letter at the newspaper? That's quite an accomplishment after writing a column for, what, ten years now?" My husband ducked away before my fist could connect with his upper arm.

"I've written the column for six years, smart aleck, and this isn't my first fan letter—I've gotten three other ones." I handed Ed the package. "The letter came with this."

He took the small box from my hands and shook it over the counter. The contents landed with a clink on the tile. Ed could no longer suppress the urge to roll his eyes. "Wow, now I am impressed. A reader has given you toenail clippers."

"Doggie toe-nail clippers," I clarified. "For Puzzle."

He looked blank.

"For the dog." I motioned to the backyard, where the stray beagle sprawled on the picnic table.

"You've named her? I told you we couldn't keep her. She's someone's pet."

"Matt named her Puzzle because of the markings on her back. They look like jigsaw pieces. Cute, huh?" I opened the sliding door and stepped outside.

"You're a cat person. You don't even like dogs," he said.

"Well, I like this dog. Come, girl! Come, Puzzle! I've got a present for you!"

The beagle lay on her back on the picnic table with all four paws pointed to heaven, looking for all her worth like road kill. At the sound of my voice, she yawned widely and thumped her tail but stayed put.

Ed followed me across the patio. "She's so lazy she doesn't even come when you call her."

"She's still weak from hunger," I replied.

I strolled to the table and sat on the bench. Puzzle's tail thumped wildly, but she made no effort to sit up. I didn't blame her. It was a beautiful summer evening, perfect for lolling around outside, doing nothing. Matt was playing with the kids next door but was due home any minute. Maybe we'd take Puzzle for a walk. Or teach her how to sit or roll over. She obviously had already perfected the command to lie down.

"We can't keep her," Ed said.

The dog ignored him, and so did I. She looked at me with chocolate eyes that were both comical and sad. Her only identifying mark was the bony lump on her left leg. I rubbed it. Her tail wagged even faster. I wondered who had allowed this sweet animal to wander with no collar or tag. I had asked that question in my last two weekly columns, but no one had come forth to claim her. Only Dorothy, who'd written all four of my fan letters, had responded. Her cocker spaniel, Rusty, had recently died. The toenail clippers were Rusty's, and she couldn't bear the sight of them anymore.

Puzzle rolled to her side and pawed my arm. Her toenails were long enough to paint, but I had no idea how to use the clippers. I would ask the veterinarian when I took her for a checkup. I rubbed her ears and dodged the tongue that sought my cheek. She had terrible breath, but we'd take care of that too. On Saturday, Matt and I would shop in the city for a collar, toys, and special treats that were good for halitosis. My dog-owner friends at the newspaper had helped me make a list of essentials.

"We can't keep her," Ed repeated. "She belongs to someone."

"Hush, Matt will hear you," I whispered.

I waved to our son as he scampered across the neighbor's driveway. Hearing him, or perhaps smelling him, Puzzle bolted from the table as though shot from a cannon. Barking happily, she bounded across the grass and jumped on Matt's chest, knocking him on his rear. They rolled around on the lawn. Laughing, Matt struggled to his feet and stumbled toward us as Puzzle grabbed the cuff of his shorts and held on.

I propped my face on my hands and sighed. "What a heartwarming sight—a boy and his dog."

"She's trying to rip his shorts right off him," Ed replied. He touched my shoulder. "Look, some other little kid might be missing Puzzle. It's not healthy to get so attached."

I shrugged off his hand. "You're wrong," I said. At least I hoped he was.

"So this is the mysterious dog I've read about," the vet said.

"Her name is Puzzle," Matt replied. He sat on the exam table with his arms wound around her neck.

"I know. This pooch is famous, because your mom wrote about her in the newspaper." Doctor

Jeff's eyes settled on mine. "I pinned your column on the bulletin board in the lobby, in case one of my patients is missing a beagle."

"Oh, good idea," I said around the lump in my throat.

"She's my doggie," Matt said.

Doctor Jeff smiled. He lifted Matt off the examination table and set him on the floor, patted his head, and turned back to Puzzle.

"See this knob? She's had a broken leg bone that's healed over," Doctor Jeff said. He positioned Puzzle on her side and lifted her back leg. She complied completely, as though she had done this a hundred times before. "She's been spayed. There are a lot of other scars on her belly, though. I think she's been on the loose for a while. Strays get scratched up when they run through barbed-wire fences. And her gums are in bad shape. Bad diet or malnutrition is my guess."

"Maybe her owners didn't feed her," I said stiffly.

"Or she could have been lost and wandering around looking for them," Doctor Jeff said.

"Or they threw her away like garbage."

Doctor Jeff put his hand on my mine, but I couldn't meet his gaze. "You did the right thing taking her in and bringing her here. We'll give her immunizations and medicine for her gums. If no one claims her, then she'll have a good home with you."

"I know," I said, but his words didn't comfort me. Puzzle wasn't really ours. Not yet, anyway.

In the lobby, Matt held Puzzle on a leash while the receptionist admired her. After I paid the bill, I wandered over to the bulletin board and found my "That's Life" column pinned up between thank-you notes and photocopied articles about the dangers of heartworm and the importance of neutering. I pulled my column from the board and stuffed it in my pocket.

On the way home from the vet's office, I swung into a fast food joint for a quick snack. At the drive-through window the cashier took my money and handed me two vanilla cones and a plain junior hamburger.

She peered at Matt, the dog, and me, as though sizing us up. "Hey, is that Puzzle?"

My heart jumped like a fish in a bucket. Did the cashier recognize her?

"I've been reading your column in the newspaper," she explained. "Did you find her owner yet?"

"She's our doggie," Matt called from the back seat.

"Nope, no one has claimed her," I added, and handed Matt his cone.

"Well, she sure is cute. Someone must be looking for her," the cashier said.

After Puzzle wolfed down her hamburger, I gave her my ice-cream cone. I'd lost my appetite.

"Newsroom. May I help you?" I propped the receiver between my chin and shoulder and kept typing. My column was due in an hour, and I was struggling with it.

"I think I know where that beagle came from," the caller said, without introducing himself. I stopped typing mid-sentence.

"Are you Puzzle's owner?"

"Her name is Sadie. She belonged to a neighbor of ours."

I couldn't breathe. "And they want her back?"

"I doubt it; they took off. They were tenants on a place over on County Y. Couldn't pay rent, and the sheriff was always over there for one thing or the other."

I knew the road. It was three or four miles from our place, rural, with run-down houses and dilapidated barns and outbuildings. The police reporter at the paper had written many stories about problems on County Y.

"How do you know the dog I wrote about is Sadie?"

"You wrote that she had a big bump on her left leg. It was from a break. You don't want to know how the bone got broke. Anyway, I fixed up Sadie and tried to get her to stay with me and the wife. She did for a while, but she kept going back to her owners. Didn't have a lick of sense, that dog."

My hands were shaking. "You said her owners moved away?"

"Ran away is more like it. They left their animals—couple of cows, a horse, a few chickens, a bunch of cats. No one was feeding them animals, so I notified the county." The caller cleared his throat. "I would have taken in Sadie, but I couldn't find her. We were out of town for a few weeks, visiting our son in Kansas City, when her people abandoned her and the rest of them animals. Sadie must have wandered until she found someone who would feed her. Maybe that's how she came to you."

I don't know how I mustered the strength to ask, "Do you want the dog?"

"Sure, I'd like to have her, but my wife says she belongs to you now. See, it took Elsie a while to catch up on her newspapers, because we'd been away. She read about Sadie, I mean Puzzle, in your column. Elsie always reads your column. She's a fan."

I was right—Puzzle belonged with us! We could keep her with a clear conscience. She was meant to be ours. I couldn't wait to get home.

Even Ed relented when I told him about the caller.

We celebrated by taking Puzzle for a walk on a new leash. She ran down our country road, her nose pressed to the ground, with Matt galloping behind her.

I caved in to my husband's demands and stopped treating Puzzle to ice cream and hamburgers from McDonalds. He reasoned that the extra weight wasn't good for her bad leg. We got her teeth cleaned, and I learned how to trim her nails with Dorothy's doggie clippers, although she didn't like it much.

Ten weeks after Puzzle wandered into our yard, the harvest moon lit up the house like a giant nightlight. Matt cried out in his sleep and I went to check on him. As I passed the slider in the dining room, I saw Puzzle asleep on a blanket on the picnic table. She was curled up tight like a caterpillar. She didn't much care for the new doggie condo we had bought for her, and she wouldn't come inside for more than a few minutes at a time.

The next morning, she was gone.

"Beagles do that, they run off while following their nose," a coworker told me. It had been three days, and I was distraught. Matt was inconsolable. Ed felt bad, too. We missed our dog.

We drove up and down country roads with the car windows down, calling her names: Puzzle and Sadie.

On a hunch one afternoon after work, I took a detour down County Y and drove slowly past three miles of sagging farmhouses. At the end of the road, where County Y meets County A, stood an old two-story with a front porch that had seen better days.

An older man and woman sat on the porch. She was reading a newspaper and paid no attention to my old Ford. Seeing me, the man reached down and patted the head of a dog, a beagle, stretched out next to his chair. Then the man raised his hand and waved.

I knew it then: Puzzle had gone home. She was right were she belonged.

~Ellen D. Hosafros

Trouble on the Hoof

Finally! The sun was out! We were two stir-crazy nine-year-olds who had been cooped up in the house for four long summer days, watching the rain come down. I was visiting my best friend, Sally, who lived on a large farm, where cattle grazed in rolling pastures separated by barbed-wire fences and hogs wallowed in a big pen by the barn.

Sally and I spent every possible minute together. Each September we crossed our fingers and wished on every star that we would be in the same class at school. We were in the same Brownie troop, swim class, and dance class. We liked to pretend we were sisters. Summers were the best—we swam in the spring-fed creek, read Nancy Drew and the Hardy Boys, and had sleepovers every chance we got. Sally's home was just two miles down a country road from mine, so most summer mornings we would meet halfway down the road between our homes, then walk together back to one house or the other. We climbed trees, built playhouses, and hiked over the pastures with Sally's German shepherd, Bill.

Bill was the best! When Sally's older sister, Susan, got too bossy, he would jump up and put his big paws on her chest with a warning growl. If she yelled at us, Bill would push her down and flop on top of her, tongue lolling out of his mouth in a big doggie grin, while Sally and I howled with laughter, and Susan howled with indignation. There he would stay until we called him off. He was our pal and went everywhere we did. Our folks never worried about our safety as long as Bill was around, and he was always around.

It was a particularly fine summer morning, and we were more than weary of being inside. We'd spent the past few days indoors—giggling, playing Old Maid, Go Fish, paper dolls, and (our favorite) Torment the Siblings. Both sets of parents said they were ready to sell us to the gypsies. The only thing worse than having us together was having us separated and whining about it, so I had been allowed to sleep over at the farm the past two nights. At breakfast we told Sally's parents that we planned to spend the day at the creek. The farm's little creek was shallow and sluggish, with warm murky water that barely covered our toes and the tadpoles, but after a good rain, the stream would fill up and create deep, cool swimming holes.

Sally's folks agreed with our plan, and her mom reminded us (needlessly) to take Bill along. The one thing Sally's dad insisted upon that fine morning was that we stay out of the south pasture. A bull whose infected horn had been removed was penned there. This bull was a grumpy old guy on the best of days, and the operation had made him downright mean. "One horn is plenty when it comes to causing trouble," Sally's dad warned us. "I want you girls to promise me you'll stay away from him. He could really hurt you."

We cheerily agreed and bounced out of the house, the screen door slamming behind us. Blue sky was reflected in every puddle, and the air was so fresh and sweet we couldn't breathe deep enough to get it all in. We picked our way down the muddy lane to the barn with Bill loping along beside us, stopping to sniff at every dew-laden bush and clump of grass. We paused at the pigpen to gaze at the baby pigs with their pink, curly tails, but knew better than to try to touch them. Their massive black-and-white mother snorted at us and gave us a look as if to say, "Don't even think about it!"

We wandered into the barn and climbed around in the hayloft, trying to catch wild kittens, but they were too quick and too skittish for us. They would stare at us with their big blue eyes, looking so fuzzy and adorable we could hardly wait to get our hands on them, but when we reached out, they would leap away, squeezing between the hay bales where we couldn't reach them or scampering up the wooden beams with their sharp claws, far above our heads. Bill *whuffed* in boredom, slouching on the straw-covered floor below us.

The wet earth steamed like a teakettle in the sun's glare, and the loft grew stuffy and humid. The air in the barn was full of dust mites and the sweet tickle of hay. We were sneezing, sticky with sweat, itchy from rolling in the hay, and yearning for a splash in that cool water. It was time to get down to the creek and jump in. The closest way to the creek was straight through the forbidden south pasture, of course. We stood in the shaded doorway of the barn, considering our options.

"Well, I guess we could take the trail around the fence line and through the woods," Sally offered unenthusiastically.

"Y-e-a-h," I replied reluctantly. "We don't want to run into that bull. It sure is the long way around, though." I lifted my hair off the back of my sweaty neck, hoping for a breeze.

"Sure is," sighed Sally. "And it's so hot! I don't even see that bull, do you?"

We clambered up on the wooden fence and peered up and down the pasture. As far as we could see, there was no sign of a grumpy bull. Most of the field was open and grassy, except for some short, flimsy mesquite trees at the far end. We perched on the top rail, the summer sun beating down on our backs and shoulders.

"I don't see anything," I declared. "He's too big to hide behind those skimpy little trees, don't you think?"

Sally squinted down the pasture. "Maybe Dad decided to put him somewhere else, in case we forgot." She chewed on the end of one long auburn pigtail, trying that thought on for size.

"Maybe so," I agreed, gazing judiciously across the field. "There are some muddy spots, but the pasture's not nearly as bad as the trail will be. Our shoes will be covered in mud by the time we get to the creek, if we take the long way."

"That's right," said Sally, nodding her head decisively. "Mom will kill me if I get mud all over these new tennis shoes. We could cut across the corner of the field, so we won't hardly be in the pasture at all . . . just a few minutes at the most. I'm sure Dad must have moved him, 'cause I don't see that bull anywhere."

Her eyes met mine, and we both grinned.

"Let's go!" she said, grabbing my hand.

We jumped from the top rail, our feet squishing in the saturated earth as we landed. We headed for the fence on the opposite side, trying to step on the patches of grass and stay out of the mud, all the while glancing toward the far end of the pasture and keeping an eye out for the bull that probably wasn't even there, anyway.

He was. We were halfway across the field when Bill began to bark wildly and push against our legs, as if urging us on.

"Stop it, Bill," snapped Sally, swatting at him. "You're going to push us into the mud! . . . Uh-oh."

Hearing the tone in her voice, I turned to see the bull breaking out of the mesquite cover and thundering toward us at an alarming speed, his one very sharp horn pointed in our direction. We both screamed and ran for the fence, but we hit a large patch of mud that stuck to our shoes and began to build up on them, slowing us down. I quite literally ran out of my loafers, leaving them buried in the gummy black clay of the south pasture. Even so, I could tell I wasn't going to make it, and Sally's flying pigtails were only a step ahead of me.

I shut my eyes and flung myself toward the fence, rolling on the ground in hopes the bull would turn aside or jump over me. I heard a low growl and an earsplitting, furious bellow and opened my eyes to see Bill leap through the air and sink his teeth deep into the bull's nose, his weight swinging the bull's head right around in the opposite direction. Sally scrambled over the fence, and I rolled under. We crouched, breathless, peeking between the boards as the bull roared and bucked and shook his head, doing his best to dislodge that demon hanging onto his nose! He was no longer interested in us at all.

"Run, Bill, run!" we shrieked in unison, jumping up and down like mud-covered cheerleaders.

Bill let go, dropped to the ground, and led the bull on a merry chase across the pasture away from us, weaving back and forth, easily dodging that angry horn. At the far end of the pasture, he scooted under the fence and trotted back toward us, mission accomplished. The bull bellowed and snorted, tossing his head and pawing the ground where Bill had escaped.

Here came our hero, tail wagging, panting happily, a big grin on his proud, intelligent face. We hugged him and praised him and promised him every doggie treat imaginable, while he licked our faces affectionately as if to say, "No big deal. I was just doing my job."

If only he could have saved us from Sally's dad when we had to explain our muddy clothes to him. Bill got a whole bowl of Milk-Bones, and we got no sleepovers, no swimming in the creek, and no visits for a whole week. I got my muddy loafers back, and the bull got the south pasture all to himself for the rest of the summer.

~Carolyn Blankenship

For the Love of a Dog

The first time I had to prove my love, it was a painful, but very rewarding, experience. On that mild autumn afternoon in my Midwestern hometown, I experienced one of those coming-of-age transformations you might read about in a book.

Although I rarely found myself home alone, my parents, two brothers, and sister had gone shopping, and I was left behind to study for a test. As I sat alone at the dining room table, I debated between going to ride my bike and studying the next three chapters in my seventh grade English book. A loud yelp pierced the silence.

My golden retriever let out a mournful howl, which I could hear as if he were beside me. Jumping up, I walked quickly to the back window. Champ's barking was much louder as I entered the kitchen.

I realized his bark sounded strange. Leaning over the sink, I peered into the backyard. A bizarre scene stunned me. Champ hung upside down with his right hind leg caught in one of the top rungs of our wire-mesh fence. Panicked, I pushed away from the countertop, blasted through the backdoor, and raced across the yard. Champ yelped wildly.

Struggling to grasp how a harmless, waist-high fence between our yard and our neighbor's had become a steel trap, I wondered whether I could help or whether I would make things worse. My heart raced as I fought panic. Could his leg be broken? Would it break if I tried to move it? Champ's painful predicament overwhelmed me, but I could not stand idle and watch as my friend suffered.

"What happened, boy?" I reached out to touch him and let him know help had arrived. I quickly drew back when he growled.

Ignoring the warning, I tried again, holding out my right hand to show I was not a threat. Champ whimpered. I moved my hand closer, inching toward his shoulder.

"It's okay, boy. We'll fix this." Confidently, I reached closer. In an instant, Champ's sharp teeth lashed out and chomped down on my fingers. Yelling a whole string of curse words, I yanked my hand away from the jaws.

"Damn! That hurt! Why did you do that, you dumb dog? Stupid dog! I'm tryin' to help ya', boy," I choked out as anger spilled from my mouth like the blood streaming from my hand.

Pain shot up my arm and tears welled up in my eyes, but I refused to wimp out. Although I was angry at Champ for getting into such a mess and for biting me so viciously, I could not leave him alone. Looking away from my injury and into Champ's glazed eyes, I realized he had to be in tremendous pain to bite me. The pressure of the moment almost paralyzed me, but I knew I had to act. I could not wait for hours until Dad came home to fix things. I decided I could put my pain on hold, hoping my buddy knew I was there to rescue him.

"I'm gonna' get ya' outta' there, boy, but it may hurt a bit."

I looked down at my wound and squeezed my hand so the trickling blood would stop. Then I sucked on the wound and spit out the blood.

Before I moved toward Champ again, I studied how his leg was caught in the fence. He was always jumping over the fence into the neighbor's yard. This time, though, he'd slipped and not cleared the top. The rectangular openings, about three inches wide, were enough to allow his leg to pass through. As Champ's weight carried him down, his hind leg twisted and wedged into the fence in a freakish accident, and the blood-stained steel ripped into his leg.

Though I knew I needed to act, I still hesitated. It ran against the grain of good sense to deliberately allow a dog to bite me. But this was my dog. This was my best friend.

Getting an idea, I ripped off my flannel shirt and wrapped it around my injured hand.

"Okay, big guy, we'll see if you can bite through this," I said as I stepped forward and reached for Champ. He snarled and bit me again, sinking his teeth into the flannel. Pain shot through my tender hand. Determined, I moved in closer, causing Champ's jaws to open. He barked and snapped wildly.

"It's okay, boy. I'm gonna help you." I was shaking, but I spoke in a soothing voice, sensing he was terrified. But it just made him start to writhe around, which I knew would only aggravate the pain.

Moving as quickly as I could, I reached my arms under Champ and felt his teeth chomping into the soft fleshy part of my exposed arm. I turned my head away from his snout to protect my face. Getting a secure hold of his body, I pressed him against my chest to bear his weight. I first lifted him a bit to lessen the pressure on his leg and then rotated him around and up to maneuver his bleeding leg through the steel trap. Champ immediately broke free from my arms and landed upright, on all fours, on the ground. I was amazed that his leg seemed all right. He limped a little, but was wagging his tail and jumping up on me.

I knelt down and put my arms around Champ, who busily licked my face. As we rolled around in the grass, the tension and the pain vanished. I knew my best friend would be okay.

As he slobbered all over my face, I remembered the first time I'd picked up the little butterscotch-colored fur ball amidst the other pups at the kennel. My heart had gone out to him. Dad had cautioned me then that being responsible for a living creature would require personal sacrifices. I'd never imagined it would require shedding blood.

I don't remember the grade on my English test the next day, but I must have passed. The bigger test had come the day before—when my heart and my friendship were on the line. My love for my dog gave me the strength to willingly sacrifice my well-being for his. Though the pain had been intense, I would do it all over again. I would follow my heart and be true to my friend, no matter what. That experience still stands as one of my life's greatest lessons.

~Dennis Jamison

Ditto, Darling

G retchen circled twice and then flopped on the floor at my side of the bed. A sigh three times bigger than her boxer body vented all her stored-up tension. Sometime in early puppyhood, our family pet had made it her life's purpose to see her people settled into bed at the end of the day.

Not that she didn't have many other things to do. A credit to her ancestors, which had been selectively bred from early eighteenth-century Germany, Gretchen was built like a coiled spring. Pushed to describe her in one word, I would have to say "effervescent." Brave and loyal, she was made for fun and play. An ambitious daily schedule kept her on the run all day long. Before the final farewell of the setting sun, she would dash across fields, visit with neighbors, bully birds at the stream, chase cows, and dodge squealing granddaughters whirling on the tire swing.

After sundown, the urgings of her own dreamland were barred by the fact that all her humans were still awake. Gretchen nudged us off to bed, one at a time. We were slow to realize the concentrated effort she put into herding us to the Land of Nod each and every evening. That loud sigh voiced her thoughts: *Phew! Finally! What a day!* Then she was off to chase wild rabbits and to howl with phantom wolves in her dreams.

Near the end of Gretchen's puppyhood, we relocated. She helped, bounding from van to house and room to room, her face alive with discovery and infectious joy. The house, set in Washington state's gorgeous orchard country, had a pull-down ladder stairway to the bedroom upstairs. Karen, our youngest, claimed dibs on the roomy attic. A string of helpers carried her belongings up the vertical staircase, organizing a choreographed group effort to get her bed and furnishings up there. Truth be told, it took a group effort to get me up there, vertigo intact. While we off-loaded furniture and boxes and bedsprings, Gretchen's fun ended at the bottom of the stairs each time we ascended into that great gaping maw.

Hubby thought it would be neat if Gretchen would climb the ladder, so he coaxed her with a bite of his banana, unsure whether the fruit would entice her. He actually thought it might take days and days and expensive steak bits to train her, but she whimpered twice and was up the stairs to nab the prize. It surprised her as much as us, especially when she turned around and looked back down. (But that's another banana.)

We taught our pet to speak too. All it took was praise and treats for every accidental noise that resembled dog talk. She spoke on request, as long as she sniffed a dog biscuit tucked in our hand. Pretty soon she assembled sounds in a string of dog language. It seemed natural for us to respond. It led to pleasant conversations, full of lively dialogue.

Oh, how I wish it were as easy training kids. Our daughter Karen, who was approaching the fringes of adulthood, stretched the boundary of our house rules to elastic fatigue on a daily basis. She worked in town, and we lived up a twisty mountain road, and it was winter. Fretting traced lines across my brow every evening from quitting time until she walked in our door. If she went out with friends afterward and didn't call me, and she often didn't, my fears spiraled up the worry scale. Driving on packed snow in subzero temperatures rated a certain level of worry, but worse was the thought of her behind the wheel during a "heat wave" thaw at thirty-two degrees, which created the slipperiest ice of all.

I always knew when Karen got home by our puppy's

standard-issue spirited "Welcome home!" Late or not, Gretchen was always just glad to see her favorite human come through the door.

Then came the night when my daughter was later than ever before. Worry escalated to near anguish. I sat up waiting, a knot in my stomach, and read (sort of) and then watched television (not really). One of my envisioned worst-case scenarios saw Karen stuck in the snow; another saw her dangling over the edge somewhere along the twenty-minute drive up our mountain road. Logic insisted that since I hadn't heard from any downhill neighbors, she probably wasn't stuck. The fire in the heater stove died to coals; the chill finally sent me to bed. Gretchen stationed herself in the doorway, her sigh still pent up inside.

It was way past two o'clock in the morning when I heard the front door close ever so gently. Gretchen came uncoiled. She unleashed her wrath in a tirade of doggy whimpers, wa-yaws, and woo-hoos. She scolded Karen for worrying us, for endangering herself, for being out far too late. And furthermore, Karen should not have been out so late on a week night, no matter how grown-up she was getting!

My errant daughter tried to shush Gretchen, but the scolding didn't stop. Gretchen's doggy harangue sounded eerily English: "Where have you been? I've been worried sick!"

I listened from the bedroom, snuggled deep in blankets. Hubby tapped my arm, and we grinned at each other like conspirators.

Gretchen dogged Karen's every step across the dark room. The verbal lashing included every word we'd taught her and a few more besides! Karen had never quite seen her unacceptable behavior in such a light. There was no doubt she'd exceeded the limits, not only in my eyes, but also in Gretchen's.

Karen headed for her stairs. By then, she was past the embarrassment of getting caught and was laughing with disbelief at the comic aspect of the scene. It got worse.

She stepped up the first two stairs. Gretchen leaped around her and beat her to the top. From the landing, the dog loomed over her like an angry mom with arms akimbo and an accusing glare. Gretchen was "in her face" all the way up the stairs.

"Okay! Okay!" Karen begged, finally contrite.

Gretchen's discipline was so effective, I didn't even need to get out of bed. From deep in my warm winter blankets, I lifted my head an inch off the pillow and hollered through the cold night air, "Ditto, darling!"

~Ginny Greene

The Anti-Alpha Male

Hey, Rhett," I rattled the leash, calling my ten-year-old golden retriever. My daughter was out on the sidewalk with the latest four-legged addition to our family. "Come see what we just got."

Although Rhett was always ready for a new adventure, the years had taken a toll on him. He'd lost his spunky physicality, so it took a moment for his pudgy body to stretch and roll. I had no idea how he would react to the feisty, energetic bundle of black Lab/spaniel puppy we'd just rescued from the local animal shelter. Originally, we'd chosen her more lethargic brother, but the humane society officer insisted that since we already had a "big, dominant male," another boy dog would never work out.

I had laughed at the officer's vision of Rhett. Never in the history of dog-dom had there been a less dominate animal. Rhett was an easygoing, roll-with-the-punches gentleman. After all, he'd grown up with two small children and a canine-controlling cat. Nonetheless, the animal officer overruled my argument, and so girlie little Taylor was ours.

Right off the bat, we figured we'd made a huge mistake. While outside on neutral ground, Taylor and Rhett had sniffed in interested camaraderie, but the instant she entered the house, fluffy, playful Taylor turned into a toothy, bouncy dominatrix. As Rhett headed for his favorite napping spot, Taylor made a flying leap onto his arthritic shoulders. She fastened her stubby paws around his neck and growled hungrily as she began to chew on his floppy ears. Poor Rhett scarcely knew what had hit him. He fell to the floor, desperately trying to see what was going on. Her razor-sharp puppy teeth must have hurt him, although he made no attempt to stop her.

"Shake her off, Rhett," I instructed. "Bite her back. Show her who's boss."

But he didn't make a move. Instead, he laid there suffering her enthusiastic teething. Stunned by his submissive behavior, I belatedly came to his rescue and pried Taylor from his head while reprimanding her. Before she could tackle him again, I gave each of them a doggie cookie. Once more the little dog was too fast as she greedily grabbed both treats and landed, spread-eagle, on Rhett's back to demolish them. Rhett had always enjoyed those biscuits, and I expected some sort of retaliation for the young mutt's thievery. Rhett, however, appeared not to mind. In fact, he seemed almost glad for the momentary respite he got while she crunched in a puppy-feeding frenzy. When I sympathetically offered Rhett a replacement treat, he openly let Taylor steal it.

Thirty minutes in the household, and Taylor had proved to be not only totally un-girly, but also bold and territorial. Fifteen minutes after that, we learned she hadn't been potty trained yet. Finally, Rhett stood up. He neared the offensive pile as if it were the most disgusting thing he'd ever witnessed. When Taylor tried to avert his attention by nipping at his tail, he lifted it out of her reach and stood stock still. His eyes bore into hers. Every time she tried to look away, he got into her face, made her pay attention. It worked. Chastised, Taylor's happy tail drooped, her head bowed heartbreakingly low. Rhett walked regally to the door and gave a discreet grunt, signaling to me that he wanted out. The puppy, head still lowered, followed him outside and watched attentively as Rhett did his business. Patiently, he waited for her to do the same. She did. Taylor never forgot her lesson and never again made a mess inside the house. Never.

"Good boy, Rhett." I scratched his chin, rewarding him for a job well done. I was relieved he'd made his stand.

A heartbeat later, though, Taylor knocked his head out of the way so that she could receive this praise as well. I scooped her up in one arm, anxious to pet my old mistreated dog. But he had already collapsed in an exhausted heap, where he remained for an hour or so, too tired to do anything else.

During the next few days, Taylor continued on her merry, "Rhett-abusing way." Her favorite pastime was attacking the big, dominate male until she fell asleep on his ribs. True to his nature, Rhett would simply lie there, afraid to move. She slobbered on his toys; she pushed him around until I wanted to howl. She ran him ragged and grabbed all the attention for herself. She kept all the cookies too.

Repeatedly, I told Rhett, even showed him how, to tell Taylor no, to push her back, to be forceful and in control. But he refused. The last straw for me came when I realized that she was taking his food as well. The instant I put down food for them, she would race between Rhett's legs, gobble his grown-up food in a trice, then duck back under his stomach and proceed to wolf down her puppy chow. Again, I told Rhett to show some muscle; again he refused. I called the vet.

"Don't worry," the vet assured me. "Let them go. Just don't give Rhett any extra food. Once he gets hungry enough, he'll step on her toes and teach her to behave."

Fine. I gave the family strict instructions that under no circumstances whatsoever were they to give Rhett any munchies. There was to be no "accidentally on purpose" meat droppings at the dinner table; no "Oh, that ham sandwich slipped out of my fingers!" I was adamant: No food for Rhett except his usual kibble. His big, soulful, brown eyes made it hard to be strong, but I was.

Despite my vigilance, this ruse backfired too. Now the big dominant male didn't even bother to go to his bowl; he just flopped down in the hallway and watched the little monster pup gobble every morsel in sight. It was true that this self-imposed diet was trimming Rhett's roly-poly physique a bit. That and the extra puppy-inspired exercise were undoubtedly healthy for him. Meanwhile, though, Taylor was developing a belly that nearly dragged on the floor, and she could barely run.

I didn't understand what was happening, until one day my son declared that we'd run out of hot dogs. He didn't even like hot dogs! When my husband responded to the announcement as if the end of the world was near, I saw the light. Before they could race out the door to the grocery, I called a family meeting.

"You guys are feeding Rhett, aren't you?"

Three heads bowed in shame. Even Rhett looked guilty. Taylor was too busy biting Rhett's ankles to notice.

"Okay, that does it!" I growled, angrily. "From now on, I'm in charge of all things dog in this house."

I was brutal too. When Taylor nudged Rhett out of his bed, I shoved her out onto the cold kitchen floor. When she chewed his ears till mine hurt, I unlocked her jaw and snarled in her face. When she stole his cookies, I yanked them out of her mouth and threw them in the trash. Now, at last, it was Taylor who didn't know what hit her. In a few short hours, she learned to ease up on Rhett and to respect me. Of course, the true test came that evening at suppertime.

As usual, I filled two bowls, one with puppy chow and the other with senior dog food. Bracing myself against Taylor's exuberant nosh fest, I set the dishes on the floor. The instant Taylor stuck her nose into Rhett's bowl, I grabbed her and lugged her startled, fat body into the middle of the room—far away from the food. A nanosecond later, she waddled back.

"Taylor, no!" I hollered. "No food! No, Taylor, no!" I flattened her tubby rump onto the floor and made her sit and stay. She whimpered and wiggled, but I refused to let her up. Once she understood, I marched over to Rhett, where he lay terrified by my unaccustomed loudness. I yanked him up and literally had to drag him to his dinner. Honestly, I had to force the chunks of kibble into his mouth. When he finally took a few bites on his own, I petted him profusely, praising the heck out of him. "Rhett, eat. Good boy, Rhett. Eat your good food."

Taylor, thinking everything was back to normal, started toward us, and I nailed her again. "Taylor! Bad dog. Sit."

And she did. Sure, she worried and wobbled and wagged her tail, but she didn't get up. I was feeling pretty cocky. Rhett was eating, Taylor was waiting, and I was tougher than I ever dreamed I could be.

Then an odd thing happened. Rhett took a huge, cheek-puffing mouthful of food. There was so much kibble stuffed into his mouth that his face ballooned out over his lips. Slowly, he walked over to Taylor, fixed his compassionate golden retriever eyes on me, and then spat the whole soggy mess onto the floor in front of his chubby little buddy. She impatiently awaited my signal but didn't move.

"Rhett," I explained, nearly pleading with him. "You have to eat. Human food is not good for you, and too much of any food isn't good for the puppy."

But his eyes told a different story. They seemed to say, "She's a baby. How can we expect her to grow up big and strong, if we don't give her everything she needs?"

"That's true," I nodded in empathy. "Still, you need to eat too. We must teach her to share."

Call me crazy, but I swear he agreed with my logic. I patted him on the head and let the ravenous Taylor consume the food Rhett had given her. Rhett sighed heavily and flopped on the floor.

It took about three months before I could trust Taylor and Rhett to eat alone properly. During that time, my daughter and I took turns feeding the dogs by standing guard between them until Rhett had eaten his fill. Only then did we allow Taylor to finish up his leftovers. And that big dominate male always left plenty.

~Loy Michael Cerf

Some Kind of Wonderful

What kind of dog is that?" I'm often asked when I have my Furry Murry out in public. "He's a ditz," I usually say.

When choosing a dog, my husband's allergies required we get a non-shedding breed. We picked a soft-coated wheaten terrier, a breed touted for its hypoallergenic coat and for being both "intelligent and exuberant." Although our wheaten makes exuberance an art form, he is by no means an intellectual.

How this dumb but lovable creature came to be a part of our family is hard to explain. Even though I've been a dog lover all my life, I knew I shouldn't have one. Not with my yard so small and my schedule so hectic and my commute to work so long. It just didn't make sense. For years, I would make do by visiting my parents' pooches and occasionally coaxing neighborhood dogs in for a snack and a scratch.

Then, in an instant, my life was turned upside down in the worst possible way. And even though my yard was still small and my schedule still hectic and my commute just as far, I realized a dog was exactly what we needed.

Perhaps Murry's goofiness was something we needed too.

Murry is bright enough that he understands many words, but he suffers from a condition called "selective deafness." (A condition that afflicts only males and is not restricted to canines.) Calling Murry's name when food is involved enables him to transport himself in *Star Trek*-like fashion from wherever he is to wherever I am. I can whisper his name, and he hears and arrives instantaneously. But call his name repeatedly and at full volume when it's time to leave for work, and the deafness strikes. He pretends to be sleeping, eyes squeezed tightly shut, like a child feigning sleep, apparently thinking, "She won't want to disturb me."

But disturb him I do, regularly carrying his limp body to the sunroom for the day, lest he eat the house while we're gone. You see, along with Murry's selective deafness is another condition, one that causes phrases I speak to be interpreted completely opposite of how they're intended. For example:

What I say: "Stay out of my closet, Murry. Do not eat my shoes."

What Murry hears: "Welcome to the smorgasbord. Our special this evening is black leather pumps."

Although I've had many dogs in my life, I was still somewhat naive about the amount of dirt a long-haired four-legger would add. I didn't realize it meant I'd be spending the next fifteen years or so gradually transferring all the dirt and leaves from my backyard to a landfill—one vacuum cleaner bag at a time.

Freshly bathed, Murry resembles an experiment in electrocution gone wrong. Described by my daughter as having "happy hair," he looks like one of the Muppets. Although he's only 40-ish pounds (heavy on the "ish"), Murry's paws are tremendous, each about the size of a mop-head. Each autumn he uses those paws to redistribute leaves from outside to inside, four furry mop-head pawfuls at a time.

Although there's more dirt in the house since Murry arrived, there's also more laughter. Much more. While I wouldn't say it's impossible to be depressed with him around, it's definitely not easy to stay that way. He's brought such companionship and devotion. And pain.

Much like my dog, I'm neither graceful nor coordinated. This I generally blame on my feet. If I were tall, their largeness might make sense, but since I'm not, my long, narrow feet make me look like I'm preparing to ski. Because I've been maneuvering through life on these ski-feet for forty-two years, some might suppose me to be a natural at hitting the slopes. But that's where my lack of coordination comes into play.

The slope I recently faced wasn't in some luxurious ski resort, but rather my own backyard, which is a series of upward slopes. My backdoor opens onto a small deck, which is at the base of a steep incline about a dozen feet high. The yard is briefly level, then shoots steeply upward again. In the summer, it's a real joy to mow, made even more joyful by a drainage problem that's been turning parts of the yard into a swamp.

In the winter, it's even better. It's ice.

Okay, so we've got an uncoordinated person with big feet and a steep backyard that's both swampy and icy. What else do we need? A dog. A big, shaggy, dumb dog.

As I mentioned earlier, Murry was blessed with the gift of enthusiasm. He leaps into life. In fact, he leaps everywhere. Sometimes just looking at him causes him to pop straight off the ground into the air. There's no method to his madness. It's simply madness.

One recent morning, before daylight, I put Murry out back on his lead-line, which runs from the house far up onto the hill. As our yard is always heavily shaded, it was still frozen in spots in spite of recent warming. Murry barreled across the ice, up the steepest slope, to the top, then inexplicably popped into the air and got his lead-line tangled in a bush. He tried to free himself but to no avail. He was hopelessly stuck.

I begrudgingly added a coat to my nightgown-and-slipper ensemble, then headed up to rescue Murry. The icy ground crunched and sunk under each step. Frozen on top, mud underneath. Its soft-ness made climbing the grade manageable, in spite of the ice. I soon reached and freed Murry, who showed his appreciation by going airborne again. Unfortu-nately, instead of a bush, this time Murry tangled in me, knocking me onto my backside. At the top of a steep, muddy, icy slope.

I shot down that slope at speeds rivaling those of an Olympic bobsledding team, going so fast that once I reached the level area, I barely slowed before heading down the next slope and into the rail of my deck. Mud and ice filled the back of my nightgown, oozed from my shoes, matted my hair.

When I finally came to a stop, I struggled to my feet and looked up at the hill from whence I'd just come, and saw that in my wake, I'd left a trench. A butt rut.

In the days after my rapid descent through my yard, I noticed my impromptu trenching project seemed to have diverted ground water from running onto my deck. While it didn't completely fix the problem, I'm thinking a few more runs down the pike might do the trick. It was, you realize, a coordinated effort. From two who are not.

Although I've spent many words on the many messy and maddening moments with Murry, I'm as devoted to him as he is to me. I have only one regret: I wish he hadn't come from a breeder. I wish I could say that I saved him from a shelter or a neglectful owner or impending death on a freeway. I wish we'd come together in some dramatic way, because then we'd be even. But we aren't.

Murry was the one who saved me. He saved me from sorrow. Saved my little girl too. Taught both of us how to laugh and love all over again. Before Murry came, our house had become too quiet, too sad. Celeste and I were both deep in mourning over the death of my second-born, six-month-old daughter, followed a few weeks later by my husband moving out.

In the weeks that followed, Celeste distracted herself with school, dance class, and friends, while

I stumbled around, trying to immerse myself in work and a million suddenly urgent projects around the house. But even with my hammering and Celeste's nonstop chatter, there was an underlying quiet. A missing, sweet commotion.

A solution seemed suddenly obvious. We needed a dog.

When an aunt called to see how we were doing, she said those oft-spoken words, "Is there anything we can do?"

I think I surprised her by saying there was. "Find us a puppy like yours."

Before I knew it, the bouncing tan fur ball was here.

From the very beginning, Murry was everything I could have hoped for—affectionate, gentle, and endlessly patient. Best of all, though, was how he forced us to laugh. Laughter was still so painful back then. Before Murry, on the rare occasions when I'd catch myself laughing, guilt would set in. It felt wrong to enjoy anything. Other times the laughter felt false, like something I made myself do so my friends would think I was fine.

But hearing Celeste's genuine giggle as our pooch rolled her about on the floor, watching that high-stepping, clumsy puppy prance as he followed us from room to room, and getting nuzzled by a cold nose and sloppy wet muzzle forced smiles that weren't fake.

No matter how wonderful the dog, it can never take the place of a child. But in losing Camille, I learned that when you do manage to find something good, you should hold on to it as tightly as you can. Murry certainly doesn't seem to mind all the holding. Something I could never say about our fish.

~Karin Fuller

The Major

My gran was clearly the boss of not only eight-year-old me and my younger brother, Tommy, but also of our mom and dad too. At almost five feet tall and barely 100 pounds, she was the lieutenant of the household ranks and of the world at large. Neighbors and shopkeepers would not dare to contradict Gran. Behind her back, we all clicked our heels and saluted her. She'd earned the commission.

At nine years old and knowing not a word of English, Gran began spinning cotton in the Amoskeag Mills in Manchester, New Hampshire. She'd also lived through the Great Depression. She was widely admired for her compassion, intelligence, industriousness, organization, resourcefulness, and pragmatism. According to Gran, the worst sins were laziness and waste. She'd have neither in her household.

Gran never actually said no to anything. Instead, she would fiercely ask, "Are you crazy?"

And a pet was out of the question. After all, animals eat, and that costs money. A dog in the house? She'd never heard of such a wasteful and inconvenient proposal. Who would pay for its food? Who would train it and walk it? Dogs had their place and usefulness on farms, as shepherds or as watchdogs, guarding chicken coops. Just because the neighbors were wasteful and silly and kept a dog in a city apartment didn't give us cause to indulge in the same frivolousness. Then it came: "Are you crazy?" And that was that. It was no use appealing to Mom and Dad. Tommy and I knew it was all over, and we hoisted the white flag.

Gran pounded on the door and hollered, "Let me in." We figured she'd misplaced her key. So when she lugged an injured puppy into the kitchen, Tommy and I didn't know what to think.

"Tossed out of the car window. They threw him like a sack of trash and sped off. Poor little runt, and with a bum leg. Lord have mercy." She grabbed a blanket and prepared a bowl of cream of wheat and patted him down with a towel. "And in the rain. How can people sink so low?"

Tommy and I couldn't say a word. It seemed like a dream.

"Priscilla, get a bowl of water and some newspapers." I was dumbfounded. "Now. Move, missy!"

A telephone, of course, was also wasteful and unnecessary. It was late, so Gran decided she would wait until morning to go to Simione's store and use the pay phone to call the Angell Memorial Animal Rescue League of Boston. Her friend Alice sent some kittens there last summer, and they even picked them up in a van. No charge. It couldn't be easier.

Next morning she asked Alice how long it took to place the kittens and was surprised when Alice said, "Oh, only the bright orange, striped one was placed. They had to kill the other two, the puny ones. You know, with a shot." Gran's face drained and Alice assured her, "Marie, don't worry. They don't charge for it." Still, the color didn't restore to Gran's face.

It was getting late, and Tommy and I had to take the subway early the next morning to Haymarket Square for the weekly grocery shopping. After ten o'clock, the cheapest cuts of meat dwindled and the day old bread was gone. What was taking Gran so long to get ready?

We went back into the house and found her in the kitchen, putting down a line of newspapers. The black pup was tied to a leg of the gas stove. His bowls of food and water were neatly placed. Gran was twisting a couple of holey socks together to form a knot. She dangled the socks in front of the pup, and he grabbed on fiercely and shook his head and hummed a playful growl. We could almost jig to it. We witnessed a rarity that morning: Gran was laughing.

"That's right, boy. This is your chew toy. Shoes and slippers are off-limits."

Was the world coming to an end?

"Watch this, kids." She stretched out her hand. "Shake, boy, shake." He lifted his paw, and Gran announced triumphantly, "Such a smart dog!"

She noticed Tommy and me eyeballing the scene and explained, "Animals need routine and discipline, just like we do. They need order. See how quickly he learned to shake hands. In a day, he could be trained to do his duties outdoors. In a day. Today, in fact."

It turned out that Tommy and I were on our own at the markets. Trying to figure out what was happening in my world, I asked, "Gran, aren't we going to Simione's to call Angell Memorial?"

It took her off-guard, but she had a quick save. "And I've always believed you are such a smart girl, Priscilla. Are you crazy?"

Our lieutenant stepped aside and made way for the major that morning, and that name stuck for our mutt. Dad gave Major the once over and said, "You've moved a mountain, boy. My hat's off to you."

Major loved us unconditionally; and he was our confidant, playmate, and faithful friend. Gran always took him for his walk just before bedtime, and she always looked a little younger when they came back.

Seven years after he came into our lives, Major died. Tommy and I were absent from school that day and the next, and the neighbors contacted the truant officer. He admonished Gran, "These children must attend school tomorrow." The poor guy had no idea how ridiculous his proposal was or what he was bumping up against. His white flag was about to unfurl. Gran squared off, stomped her tiny foot, set her jaw, and resolved, "My grandchildren shall be absent from school the rest of the week, sir. We've had a death in the family. Show some respect." He had no quick save, and she finished him off with "Are you crazy?"

~Priscilla Carr

Blind Trust

Never run with your dog." That was the advice from the trainer. "When you're holding onto that harness, he needs to be in control, and if you run, he doesn't have enough time to control your reactions."

Of course, I ignored that advice. I liked being in control. I liked running up one of the hills in my urban neighborhood. Rising gently along a side street, it gave me a challenge without overtaxing me. My daily jog up that incline made me feel strong, in control of at least part of my life, and, above all, normal, despite the fact that I held the harness of a guide dog.

The day started out no differently than any other. A light mist lent coolness to the day and brought out the scents of pine and lilac. In running shoes and shorts, I left my apartment and headed up the street at my usual brisk pace with Raider, my golden retriever, trotting at my side. At four years old, he was in prime condition. At twenty-seven, I wanted to stay in prime condition. A little matter of not being able to see should never stop me from anything.

Raider and I rounded the corner, and I "hupped" him up. We charged up the hill. Five yards. Ten yards. My feet skimmed over cracks and humps of concrete. Raider jerked me hard to the left; I didn't follow. I didn't have time because I was running and taking control, as I'd been instructed not to do.

I went face-first into a steel pole. Then landed flat on my back on the sidewalk.

"Woof! Woof! Woof!" Raider's bark rang echoed off of the houses, a clear cry of "Help! Help! Help!"

Speech, let alone cries for help, proved beyond my ability. With my nose broken and bleeding, I could do nothing to help myself. I couldn't even control my dog. Somewhere in my fall, I'd lost hold of leash and harness. No matter. Raider stood beside me, calling for someone to pay attention and bring us aid. People came.

"Will he bite me if I come close to you?" a woman asked.

"No." That was as much as I could manage with my nose swelling to the size, and more than likely the color, of a plum.

"I called an ambulance." A second woman knelt beside me and pressed a cool, wet washcloth against my face. "Can you breathe?"

"Sort of."

I hoped I would not drown in my own blood. Strangers made sure I didn't. Having responded to Raider's pleas for help, the two women stayed with me until the paramedics arrived. Raider stayed too. Once help arrived in human form, he settled down beside me, a small golden retriever at sixty pounds, as red as a copper teakettle, my guide and, at that moment, my guardian.

He would not leave my side even when the paramedics lifted me onto a stretcher. As though he performed the trick every day, he hopped into the back of the ambulance and sat beside the gurney, his chin next to my hand. I felt his eyes upon me, watching, comforting.

At the emergency room, no one even thought to separate Raider from my side. Hospital personnel lifted me on a bed too high for Raider to touch me or for me to hold onto his leash, but he sat next to it like a sentry.

"Can you move him elsewhere?" The nurse needed Raider out of her way. He simply looked at her, she told me, and she laughed. "Okay, I'll go to the other side."

Questions were asked about insurance and all

that, an icepack applied to my nose, and then everyone left me alone until the doctor was available. I did not have a life-threatening condition, so I was not top priority in the busy city hospital. Or so they presumed, under the circumstances. It was only a broken nose.

But I began to shiver. The world commenced to tilt and spin. Sound faded in and out. I fumbled for a call button, knowing something was wrong, but could find none. My hands would not work right anyway, so it may have been only a few inches away.

"Someone help me?" I thought I called out.

No one responded. Flat on my back and out of control of my body's reactions to trauma, I could do nothing to help myself. But Raider wasn't out of his ability to control the situation. All of a sudden, I heard the *click, click, click* of doggy toenails on tile.

"Oh no, there's the dog running down the hall." The person sounded concerned, alarmed.

"Raider, come." I did not know what would happen to my dog if someone caught him and placed him far away from me. What if he ran out the automatic doors and ended up on a dangerous street? Smart as he was, he was a dog, and I could do nothing to stop him.

I tried to get out of bed. Futile. Dizziness plagued

me while lying flat. Half upright, I felt the world spinning into blackness.

"Oh no, the dog." Someone else sounded upset, as well he should, to have a dog loose in an emergency room. "Somebody—wait, I know where you came from. You go back and tell her I'll be right there."

Click. Click. Click. Nails on tiles again. Paws on the edge of the bed. A warm tongue on my cheek. "The doctor is coming." Of course, Raider could not say that, but the message came through loud and clear.

Moments later, the doctor did indeed come into my cubicle. "She's going into shock."

His words frightened me. I knew people died from shock. The doctor's announcement galvanized the ER staff into action. Someone wrapped me in a hot blanket. Another person started an intravenous line in my arm. Everything else became a blur until the plastic surgeon arrived to reset my nose. Raider sat beside my bed the whole time.

In picking a doctor out of everyone in the emergency room, Raider had very possibly saved my life. By seizing control when I was flat on my back, he had shown me that sometimes I had to trust others to assist me on my journey of independence—even if the help came in the way of a four-footed being.

~*Laurie Alice Skonicki-Eakes*

The Escape Artist

I guarantee this will keep your dog from escaping."
Across the pet store's linoleum floor, the sales clerk unfurled part of a 5' × 30' mesh dog run. The clerk's fleshy face burned red with the effort.

"Maybe, maybe not," I said. "Can we return it if it fails?"

"You did say you had a six-pound dog, right?" He failed to contain the scorn from his voice.

"Yes, but can we return it if it doesn't work?"

"Sure." He shook his head in exasperation.

Later that day when my husband helped me unload the roll of fencing from my soccer-mom mini-van, he laughed. "Overkill, don't you think, honey?"

I ignored his sarcasm while we struggled with the unwieldy roll. We lugged it around the house into the backyard.

"Okay, now where do you want to put this monstrosity?"

"Under the cedar trees, I think. Shade in the summer and some rain protection in the winter."

When we unrolled the fencing, it did look a bit much for a toy poodle, but so far she'd lived up to her given name, Mischief. The dog had proven to be wily and cunning.

Both of us struggled to keep the cumbersome metal upright. My husband anchored the circular dog run with a series of stakes. He tested its sturdiness with several tugs.

"If this doesn't hold her . . ."

"Nothing will," I said, completing his sentence as wives often do.

When we stepped back and saw the completed structure sheltered by the Pacific Northwest cedars, I thought to myself that it did appear to be excessive. It was certainly an eyesore too. Still I felt a sense of relief. Mischief's safety was my primary concern.

Sad memories of another dog heightened my frustration and worry. One Thanksgiving, my childhood pet, a toy poodle named Pepé, maneuvered his way between my aunt's gate and fence post. Before I could catch him, he raced down the alley. I became one hysterical thirteen-year-old as I ran after him. He ran only faster. To him, it was game time. I lost sight of him. Sobbing and out of breath, I returned to the family gathering.

Frantic and fearful aunts, uncles, cousins, and grandparents searched the surrounding neighborhood. The unsuccessful foot canvas spurred Dad, Mom, and me to pile into the family car and drive the streets. A sense of hopelessness sucked the air from the sedan's interior. When the car turned onto a busy thoroughfare, my pulse quickened. I couldn't bear to look at the pavement. Cars whizzed by as thoughts of "what if" silenced me.

Then I saw him, his white fluff shivering as he stood frozen and unmoving on the grassy center median. "There he is!" I yelled.

My dad braked and turned on the hazard lights. As horns honked, I jumped from the car and backtracked to the frightened dog. When I leaned down, Pepé jumped into my outstretched arms. Once his shaking stopped, I cried with relief, and he licked my tears away.

Months later, Pepé slid out the front door past a delivery man and ran into the street. That time, there was no happy ending. Determined that Mischief would not meet a similar fate, the dog run loomed in the yard.

We had adopted Mischief at Christmas and spent several days trying to find the perfect name for our new puppy, who was pitch black, fluffy, and tiny. Name suggestions included Midnight, Magic, Midget, and Blackie. The name debate continued until the pup's personality revealed itself. She shredded Christmas paper, untied ribbons and shoelaces, batted down tree ornaments, and lapped water from the tree stand. By unanimous vote, she was dubbed Mischief. I wondered now if that name had influenced her ongoing behavior. To cordon her off from Christmas packages, everyone's shoes, and other temptations, we had erected baby gates—which the two-pound, black, fuzzy puppy scaled immediately. Finally, Plexiglas affixed to the gates did the trick. Much to her dismay, her nails failed to grasp the slick surface.

In the following months, she slid beneath the garden gate. So we added chicken wire that extended from the bottom of the gate to the concrete. That same wire covered a knot hole on a wooden fence plank, which she had shimmied through, as well as several getaway sections at the fence's base, which she had crawled through.

Now, my nine-year-old daughter glared at the backyard's newest addition and said, "It looks like a prison." She shielded Mischief's eyes by curling the dog into the folds of her voluminous sweatshirt.

"Let's test it out," my husband said.

"Not yet. Mischief's going to help me with my homework." Daughter and dog scurried upstairs.

That evening my son, age ten, hovered while Mischief visited the pen. He eyed the enclosure with horror and commented that it wasn't fair to trap his dog in a torture chamber.

The next day when I could avoid the scrutiny of an amused husband and two adolescent critics, I set Mischief inside the dog run and left the yard. I stood watching at the kitchen window while she sniffed, explored, rolled onto her back, and then marked her territory.

An hour later, when I went to pick her up, she stretched all of her twenty-four inches up the fence, ready for me to lift her. She licked my hand with enthusiasm. "See, she's fine with it," I said out loud. Of course, there was no one else there to nod their approval.

All went well until the fourth day. The doorbell rang, and I chatted for a few minutes with a neighbor about an upcoming block party. When I returned to the kitchen and looked out the back door, I saw Mischief careen over the top of the dog run.

"Impossible," my husband said that evening.

"I saw her myself."

Disbelief clouded his eyes as he carried her outside to the metal cage. She plopped onto the grass, sniffed, and then curled into a black, fuzzy ball.

At dinner the conversation strayed to my overactive imagination. When the laughter subsided, we heard the doggie door open. Mischief sashayed into the kitchen.

Fortunately, Mischief has transferred her challenges to new avenues. She remains safe, and the pet store clerk remains incredulous.

~Sharyn L. Bolton

My Saving Grace

I finished my riding lesson shortly after noon, grabbed Cinder, my toy poodle, and headed for the trail. It was one of the first days of spring. The warm afternoon sun melted away the winter chill. The vibrant green of new growth contrasted with the dark evergreens, and the grass was twice as high as Cinder.

Cinder trotted briskly beside me as I powered my wheelchair along the bumpy dirt road, her long wavy ears blowing back, exposing a look of profound contentment. Since she was familiar with the route, I'd let Cinder off her leash, so she could explore. She'd disappear into the tall grass and enthusiastically dart in and out while hunting imaginary prey. Every so often she'd run back to me and look up with that silly grin and expectant look in her big brown eyes.

Watching her carefree meanderings lifted my spirits, and I forgot my own physical limitations.

That day we were taking the less-traveled route up a steep hill. As we approached the top, I noticed a lone dog loping toward us. He looked small and unassuming, so we cautiously continued in his direction, and he in ours. I soon realized that he wasn't that small and looked suspiciously like a coyote. We'd taken this trail for years without incident, so I didn't expect to come face-to-face with a wild animal, especially this close to civilization, but I decided to trust my instincts.

I called Cinder as calmly as possible, trying to get her attention before she noticed the potential danger. Having grown up with dogs, horses, and other large animals, Cinder fears nothing. If she saw the coyote, she would think it was just another dog to play with. When Cinder didn't come to my call, I tried again, struggling to keep the panic out of my voice. I knew the coyote wasn't interested in me, but Cinder is about ten pounds soaking wet, a perfect size for a snack.

The trail picks up behind Little Bit Therapeutic Riding Center, where I take horseback-riding lessons. Every week after my lesson, Cinder happily runs beside my wheelchair as we explore the trail, encountering all kinds of interesting smells and great adventures in the tall grass and woodsy terrain. On hot days, she particularly loves racing down to the creek and taking a quick dip. I wait at the top of the steep path and can't help laughing when she comes back, looking very pleased with herself, her ears dripping and her legs wet and scrawny.

Cinder was born at the riding facility, which is where we'd found each other. Before I met Cinder, I felt that caring for dogs was a huge burden and that the last thing I needed in my life was a puppy. At the same time, I was struggling with the decision of whether to end my twenty-five-year career. To my surprise, it was a very emotional decision to make, even though my disability was making it increasingly difficult to cope with the daily requirements of my job. I'd spent my entire adult life working; the thought of staying home all day, every day, terrified me. I didn't know what I'd do with myself or how I'd replace the companionship I had at the office. I was fearful that if I didn't find something to keep me occupied, I'd be lost.

Each week as I hung around the barn after my lesson, the facility manager, Taffy, brought out her dog, Mischief's, litter of puppies, two brown and three black adorable, wiggly, balls of fur. Though I enjoyed playing with the puppies, I was determined to keep my emotional distance, just as I had with

Mischief's first litter. All but one was spoken for, anyway, and as I played with that last adventurous runt of the litter, I'd tell myself it wouldn't be long before she, too, would find a home.

As the weeks passed and I spent time with the unclaimed pup, I noticed how desperately she tried to get any passerby's attention—her little tail wagging vigorously, her tiny tongue hanging out of her smiling mouth, and a look of eager anticipation on her face. In comparison, the other puppies quivered fearfully whenever strangers approached. The pup's display of friendly boldness gradually won me over, making it impossible to resist her the night she curled up in a little black ball and fell asleep on my lap, her nose tucked securely under my arm. Not long afterward, I became the anxious owner of my very first dog, whom I named Cinder.

Our first night together, I closed Cinder's crate for the night and wondered what I'd gotten myself into. As an incomplete quadriplegic living independently, I had enough challenges taking care of myself. I fell asleep fretting over how I was going to potty train a puppy and wondering what to do with her while I was at work. One consolation was Taffy's willingness to take her back if it didn't work out. *After all, she's just a dog,* I reasoned.

To my relief, things with Cinder worked themselves out. She took to potty pads fairly easily, and she quickly learned that when I left for work I would come back. I found myself looking forward to coming home to her enthusiastic greetings and to spending time playing with her. She adjusted to my wheelchair by jumping onto my lap when I needed to put on her leash or when she wanted petting, and she'd bring her toys onto a chair next to me so I could reach them for throwing. During our first week together, she learned the different sounds of my wheelchair in order to avoid getting run over. She also managed to con her way onto my bed at night rather than sleep in her crate.

I started taking Cinder for long walks in the park and at the beach, a favorite pastime I'd stopped doing when I'd ended up in the wheelchair five years earlier. Together, Cinder and I discovered new parks and trails to explore, only occasionally getting into trouble. (I still haven't figured out that my wheelchair isn't an all-terrain vehicle.) We also made many new friends during our adventures, especially when we got into trouble. With Cinder by my side, nothing seemed insurmountable, and her companionship motivated me to get out and enjoy the outdoors again.

Soon Cinder went everywhere I did, with the exception of work. I flew from Seattle to Toronto with Cinder sleeping quietly in my lap. We forded streams and climbed steep paths. Every day became an unexpected adventure. Often, we didn't even leave home before we encountered one. Continual wheelchair mishaps frequently landed me on the floor, where Cinder would curl up next to me, comforting me until help arrived in the morning.

Despite my trepidation, I made the decision to take a permanent disability leave. When the dreaded day of my "retirement" arrived, I said my tearful farewells to friends and duties, uncertain of what the future had in store for me. The next morning, a clear, crisp fall day, I took Cinder to our usual hangout along the beach. As I watched the sun's golden rays dance on the waves and Cinder chase seagulls across the sand, I felt a sense of well-being and unexpected happiness.

Three years later, I have never once looked back. Cinder and I have made the best of our newfound time together, and I've discovered a world outside the nine-to-five office walls—a big, beautiful, exciting world that Cinder has introduced to me. My saving grace at one of the most pivotal times in my life ended up being a brave and devoted black puppy.

The encounter with the coyote would now test my bravery and dedication to my loyal companion.

I called Cinder a third time, and she came closer. Frantically, I tried to grab her before she noticed the coyote, but I had difficulty reaching her from my wheelchair. Fortunately, she became interested in some smells in the grass near me, which allowed me to grab her and put her back on the leash. Crisis averted, the coyote lurked in the tall grass a little longer and then trotted off into the woods.

I kept a watchful eye in his direction and on Cinder, just to play it safe. Satisfied we were alone again, we continued up the trail a little further and then turned toward home. There, not more than twenty feet directly in front of us, right in the middle of the trail, was the coyote. This time I was certain it was a coyote, and he appeared to have no intention of leaving.

I rolled slowly in his direction, thinking the noise of my wheelchair might scare him off. Undaunted, the coyote just stood there, staring at us. I put Cinder on my lap, but I had no idea what to do next, as this was the only way home. So the coyote and I continued to stay in our respective spots, staring each other down, with Cinder on my lap, waiting impatiently to play with her new friend. I felt like a mother bear protecting her cub. The coyote would have to contend with me first, wheelchair or not;

nothing was going to hurt my puppy. The coyote finally lost interest and sauntered off into the woods. Phew, one more adventure survived by Cinder and me.

Now when we head for the trail, I tease that it's time to take "Coyote Bait" for a walk. Of course, I always keep a mother's watchful eye and a leash on my little girl. After all, my saving grace and I still have many more adventures to experience together.

~*Sue Lamoree*

The Rent Collector

F red came by for the rent," I said, as I dropped my purse and car keys on the kitchen counter.

"I already paid him. That dog!" my husband, Leonard, grumbled. He looked up from his newspaper and shook his head.

Leonard was not being derogatory. Fred *was* a dog, an old golden retriever who used to live in the house we'd bought. The hairs around his mouth and chin had gone white, but the rest of his coat remained a youthful golden red. Age had not diminished his vigor either, at least not when it came to collecting the rent.

We woke to rain on our first day in our new home, but Leonard was not going to let that interfere with his morning jog. "Not rain nor hail nor Seattle weather shall keep this avid runner from his appointed rounds," he informed me. So, bundled in Gortex and a wool cap, he set off down the long driveway—only to be stopped dead in his tracks by a barking, snarling mass of wet red fur, who made it clear to Leonard that he was going nowhere that morning. Apparently, not rain nor hail nor Seattle weather was going to keep Fred from his appointed rounds either.

Neither friend-making nor threat-making could budge that enormous lump of a dog, and there was no getting by him. Fred barked Leonard back into the house, at his heels the whole way, as the poor man attempted to maintain his dignity, striding double-time up the driveway and into the house as fast as his legs would allow. A few more choruses from Fred through the closed door persuaded us it was a good day to stay inside and unpack.

We had seen Fred at the house when we first visited with our real estate agent, and when we'd returned to double-check the floor plan, visualize our furniture within, and decide this was the house we wanted to buy. Knowing Fred had once lived here, we assumed he had wandered off from his new home in town, gotten disoriented, and accidentally returned to his old house. We called the Realtor to suggest she call the former owner to let her know where her dog was. We were sure she must be worried about her lost pet. The Realtor called back to tell us Fred was not lost after all. He had been given to a neighbor across the road, so he would not have to adjust to smaller quarters and no room to roam in his twilight years. Fred belonged in our neighborhood.

Now his aggression toward Leonard made sense. We reasoned that Fred probably had been left with the same neighbor countless times before when his owner went on vacations. If Fred thought she was just away temporarily and he still lived in our house, of course he would want to protect it from trespassers. What a good dog. Surely, it would be only a matter of days before he got used to the reality of our living in his previous home and of him living in his new home across the road.

Fred didn't see it that way. This was his house. This had been his house all his remembered life, and he didn't intend to change that now just because the lady who lived here with him had left. Over the years, he had watched the five children who had also lived here leave, until only Fred and the lady remained. Now she was gone too. But not Fred. He hadn't left with any of the others, and he wasn't leaving this time. His owner may have been willing to sell us her claim to the house, but Fred was not. This property was his turf, and he didn't intend to have us tramping all over it as if we owned it—even if we thought we did.

By late afternoon of our first day in the house, it was time to arrange the tools in the garage and set up a workshop. The garage was dark with the door closed, so we opened it to let in some sunlight. In swooped Fred, snarling and barking and leaping at us, running from one of us to the other, threatening indiscriminately, showing no favorites.

"Down boy, down," Leonard suggested from behind the carton of tools and junk in his arms, slowly backing toward the worktable at the other end of the garage.

Fred's response, loosely translated, went something like this: "Look, you jerk, I've already told you once today, get off my property. I'm not putting up with any squatters. Beat it."

We thought about showing Fred our deed to the property, the escrow papers, the bill of sale, but concluded he couldn't read and might devour them instead. The deed would then be in Fred's stomach, and possession being nine-tenths of the law, where would that leave us? We decided to negotiate. We outnumbered Fred, but he had bigger teeth.

Fred thought the house was his. We wanted to live there. Perhaps if we paid rent?

While Leonard kept Fred engaged in meaningful discussion, notwithstanding the language barrier, I slipped into the car and sped away to the supermarket, where I purchased the largest box of jumbo dog biscuits in stock.

We quickly came to terms. Fred would supply the house for us; we would supply the dog biscuits for him. Without even demanding first and last and a clean-up fee, he happily accepted the one biscuit offered and trotted out of the garage to munch it leisurely on our/his lawn. When he had finished, he rose, looked over at us approvingly, and ambled down the driveway and across the road.

We enjoyed many years in the house under this arrangement. Fred came to recognize the sound of our car coming up the street, and as we turned into the driveway we could see him bounding across the road to beat us to the door in time to collect the rent, his daily dog biscuit. Some days, when we went out separately, Fred would be there to meet each of us and collect twice. Leonard thought this was unfair, but I reasoned that since Fred didn't define ownership as we did, he probably didn't define what constituted a day—per our agreed-upon rent of one biscuit daily—the same as we did either. Besides, life was easier and quieter when we accepted Fred's definitions.

~Marcia Rudoff

Where the Need
Is Greatest

Donna could hardly control her tears as she mounted the platform at the outdoor graduation ceremony. A light breeze ruffled the flag. The audience waited, polite and attentive. The graduates sat, alert and poised. The flag had been saluted, the speeches made, the staff and students congratulated. Now it was time to take the final step and send the graduates out into the world to fulfill their mission.

Donna stopped beside one of the graduates and rested a hand on his shoulder. "Raising a puppy is an act of love and faith," she began. "When a puppy comes into your home, he comes into your heart. He is a part of your family. You give him all the time and care and love you can. Then, almost before you know it, that curious, wriggling, uncoordinated puppy has changed into an obedient, mature dog, ready to return to Guide Dogs for the Blind and take the next step in becoming the working guide.

"I'm thrilled and happy that Llama," she indicated the golden retriever next to her, "has become a working guide. But I'm sad, too, because it is always hard to say goodbye to someone you love." She picked up Llama's leash and handed it to Gil, Llama's new partner. "Goodbye, Llama. You are a special dog."

The crowd murmured in appreciation, and some in the audience sniffed audibly and reached for their tissues. Then the graduation was over. Soon Llama and Gil were on their way to Vancouver, Canada, and Donna was on her way home to Newark, California, knowing there was a good chance she would never see Llama again.

Llama was the third puppy the Hahn family—Donna, John, and their daughters Wendy and Laurel—had raised for Guide Dogs for the Blind, but he was the first to complete the program and become a working guide. He had come into their lives fifteen months earlier, a red-tinged golden retriever with white hairs on his face and muzzle that gave him a washed-out, unfinished look. "An ugly dog," Donna had said at the time. But soon his looks didn't matter.

At first, Llama was as helpless as any new baby. "Neee, neee, neee," he cried when he was left alone.

He woke Donna in the night and left yellow abstract designs on the carpet when she didn't get him out the door fast enough. Donna patiently cleaned up the accidents. Soon Llama learned to "do your business," one of the early commands that every guide dog puppy learns, and the accidents rapidly decreased.

Like all guide pups, Llama was trained with love and kind words rather than with food treats. Soon he would follow Donna through the house on his short puppy legs, collapsing at her feet when she said "Sit," happy to be rewarded with a pat and a "Good dog."

Llama seemed to double in size overnight. By the time he was five months old, he was accompanying Donna everywhere. It wasn't always easy. Llama had to learn to overcome his natural inclination to sniff the ground and greet every dog he met on the street. At the supermarket, he learned not to chase the wheels on the grocery cart. At Macy's, he learned to wait while Donna tried on clothes. With a group of other puppies in training, Llama and Donna rode the ferry across San Francisco Bay and toured the noisy city.

In May, Donna was summoned for jury duty. Of course, she took Llama. Privately, she hoped that his presence would be enough to get her automatically excused, but the plan backfired. For a week, Llama lay patiently at Donna's feet in the jury box while Donna attended the trial.

All too soon, a year was up, and the puppy that had wagged its way into Donna's heart was a full-grown dog ready to return to the Guide Dog campus in San Rafael and start professional training. There was only a fifty-fifty chance he would complete the program. Working guides must be physically and temperamentally perfect before they are entrusted with the life of a person who is blind. Donna had given Llama all the love and training she could; now his future was out of her hands.

Llama passed his physical and sailed through the training program. When it came time to be matched with a human partner, the young golden retriever was paired with Gil, a curator at an aquarium in Canada. Matching dog and human is a serious and complicated ballet in which the dog's strengths, weaknesses, and personality are balanced against the human's personality and lifestyle. When done well, an unbreakable bond of love and trust develops between human and dog.

Gil and Llama were a perfect match, and their bond grew strong and true. Gil had never had a guide dog before. Once home, he found that Llama gave him a new sense of confidence, independence, and mobility. Every day they walked together along the seawall to Gil's work in the aquarium. In time, everyone grew to know Llama, and Llama grew to know all the sights and sounds of Gil's workplace. For ten years Llama was at Gil's side every day—at home; at work; on vacation; and on trains, planes, and busses.

Meanwhile, at the Hahns', Wendy and Laurel grew up and moved away from home. John and Donna continued to raise pups. Their fourth dog became a family pet. The fifth became a working guide in Massachusetts, and the sixth a service dog for a physically handicapped teen.

While they were raising their seventh pup, Donna's husband, John, a fit and active Air Force veteran, began having stomach problems. An endoscopy revealed the bad news. John had advanced gastric cancer. Thus began a long series of treatments and operations, trying to catch the cancer that always seemed one step ahead of the surgeon's knife. It was a grim, sad, stress-filled time. Soon John could no longer take any nourishment by mouth. With John's strength waning daily, the family came to accept that he had only a few months to live.

In October, with John desperately ill, a call came from the Guide Dog placement advisor. "Donna, we just got a call that Llama is being retired. He's been working for ten years, and all that stair climbing and leading tours at the aquarium has caught up with him. He has pretty bad arthritis. Gil is coming down to train with a new dog. I know John is terribly sick, and the last thing you might want to do right now is take care of an old dog, but Gil specifically requested that we ask you if you could give Llama a retirement home. He can't keep Llama himself, but he wants him to be with someone who will love him."

"Of course we'll take him," said Donna, with no hesitation.

Several days later Donna drove up to the Guide Dog campus to pick up Llama. She paced back and forth across the receiving area as she waited for a kennel helper to bring Llama to her. "Do you think he'll recognize me after ten years?" she anxiously asked an assistant in a white lab coat.

When Llama arrived, moving stiffly in the damp morning air, it was not the joyous reunion Donna had imagined. Llama seemed pleased to see her, but in a reserved, distant way. An hour-and-a-half later, Llama was back at the house where he had spent the first year of his life.

"John, we're home." Donna pushed open the front door.

Llama didn't hesitate for a second. He walked in, turned, and headed straight into John's bedroom, as if he had been going there every day of his life. From that moment on, Llama rarely left John's bedside. Although he was too old to guide, Llama had found a place where he was needed. Llama was a careful and gentle companion for John. When John got out of bed, pushing the pole that held his intravenous feeding bottles, Llama was beside him, ready to protect him, but careful never to get in his way or get tangled in the medical apparatus.

"I don't know how that dog always seems to know exactly what you need, but he surely does," said Donna more than once.

"He was sent to take care of me," John replied.

By the end of the month, John's condition had worsened. The hospice nurse administered morphine. Donna was afraid the drug would make John disoriented and that he would try to get out of bed and fall over Llama, so she ordered the dog to leave.

"Llama, out."

Llama, who never disobeyed a command, didn't budge.

"Llama, out."

Llama didn't move a muscle and remained planted by John's bed.

The next morning, however, Llama began to pace frantically back and forth through the house.

"What's wrong with him, Mom?" asked Wendy, who had come home to help her mother.

"I don't know. Maybe he's sick."

The pacing continued all day and into the evening. At 9:30 that night, John passed away. Llama stopped pacing and lay quietly by the door.

"He must have known the end was near," said Wendy.

Llama lay at the door, refusing to move, forcing people to step over him. For three days he grieved, along with the rest of the family. Then he got up, went to Donna, and placed his grizzled head in her lap. He had found someone else who needed him.

Today, Llama and Donna are rarely separated. They visit neighborhood friends, both dog and human, daily. They go to Guide Dog meetings, take walks around the lake, and occasionally go to the beach. A neighbor has made Llama a ramp, so that he can avoid stairs and get in and out of cars. The dog Donna had given a home and her heart to and then sent out into the world to help another had brought that love back to Donna when her need was greatest.

~Tish Davidson

The Cost of a Dog

M rs. Hall, you have to get this child a dog."
I sat in the second-grade-sized chair, with
my son's latest writing effort in my lap. His teacher
was smiling, but I don't think she was kidding. After
all, she'd had my son, John, in the first grade too, and
by now she was getting sick and tired of his standard
essays. Every paper had the same theme, and considering he was just seven, even less variation:

> I want a dog. I will feed it. I will play with it. My
> mom won't let me have a dog. My mom says dogs
> are a lot of werk. I will do evrything. I reelly, reelly,
> reelly want a dog. The end.

That night I spoke to my husband about the pos-
sibility of getting a dog for John. First, we'd need to
fence the backyard, because any dog would have to

stay outside. My husband agreed. Second, we would need to consider what kind of dog would be best around children, because we had three of those. My husband approved wholeheartedly. Finally, we would need to think about the costs involved, because we lived on a pretty tight budget. My husband was one hundred percent behind me.

The key, I said, summing up the whole dog issue, was to take our time and make the right decisions, thereby ensuring the perfect pet addition to the family. It looked like my husband was listening, but he hadn't heard a word I'd said.

A few weeks later we had a fence. Boy, that was fast. I hadn't even made it to the library to check out any dog books. But there was still plenty of time for research. The spring baseball season was in full swing, so we were entirely too busy to worry about a dog. Until a puppy showed up at the ballpark one day. In the back of a truck belonging to a team member's grandfather. Hmmmm . . . it was just a little too coincidental.

"Mrs. Hall, why don't you take a look at this puppy?"

Why did I have the feeling my husband and John knew all about this puppy? My hubby glanced around sheepishly, avoiding eye contact. John, however, turned his big, brown eyes toward his mommy, looking just like, well, a puppy.

"What kind of dog is this, anyway?" I asked, only because I was raised to be polite to my elders.

The kindly grandfather thought she must be part pointer, part beagle. Pointer? I didn't know much about pointers. Come to think of it, all I knew about beagles was based on Snoopy. Did that count?

Okay, she was cute. She was a puppy; she was supposed to be cute. But I still had my research to do on breeds and training and costs. It was way too soon to make a decision about a dog.

I guess I was the only one surprised to find a brown and white ball of fur trembling in the back seat of our car that day. So much for taking our time choosing a pet.

John named her Sally Hall. Both father and son were ecstatic, their doggy prayers finally answered. I was more concerned about practical matters. Like dog food, shelter, and shots. All the stuff my husband had conveniently forgotten while loading Sally into the back seat. Well, Sally was home now; we'd have to make the best of it.

Fortunately, we have a rather large, screened-in porch, a great spot, we figured, for our new puppy. She would have plenty of fresh air, with access to our big, now fenced-in backyard. But all the helpful dog owners at the ballpark had recommended a crate for her to sleep in. Dogs like to have their own little home, they said. And she'll train almost overnight, they added. So we headed to the pet store. We bought a crate, puppy food, toys, a leash, dog treats, and a collar. Whew! We'd spent more than I'd bargained for, but that was just about everything, right?

That evening we placed Sally in the crate with one of John's baby blankets inside to keep her company. All was quiet and calm through the night. I drifted off to sleep wondering why I'd been so worried.

The following morning, I cleaned Sally's crate as well as John's baby blanket. Apparently, Sally didn't know that dogs aren't supposed to soil their own home. Next, John and I loaded her into the car for her first vet visit. It soon became clear that Sally was one of those rare breeds who do not enjoy a good road trip. She threw up before we'd even left the neighborhood.

Of course, she charmed everyone at the vet's office. While John beamed, I scribbled reams of notes. Sally would need shots (every year) and heartworm medication (every month), plus the medication for regular worms (could take several doses; uh-oh). She'd likely benefit from a dog training class, considering her breed. (That didn't sound encouraging.) And, naturally, she'd need to be spayed in a few months. The bill was more than $200, with who-knew-how-much-more in costs for future training, well care, and emergencies. So much for our children's college funds.

That evening, after thoroughly cleaning the crate again, we said our good nights to Sally. John hated leaving his dog on the porch, but I was adamant. That was my last line in the carpet, so to speak, and I had no intention of letting Sally cross it. So when the first little yips began, I coolly ignored her. The yips gave way to yelps. I turned up the volume on the TV. The pitiful puppy whining continued. I went upstairs and put on my pajamas. Then I came back downstairs to sit outside on the porch with Sally.

Sally redeemed herself when she crate-trained so quickly. She even stopped her crying through the night. But as soon as the dawning sun peeked out, she would bark. And bark. And bark. So by 6:00 A.M., everyone was up, whether they had planned to be or not. Someone (need I say it was always Mom or Dad?) would stumble downstairs and let Sally out to do her business. She'd bound from her crate and stand around for a while. This was no potty emergency; Sally had learned a new trick. Barking nonstop was sure to get our attention. It was an amazingly effective alarm clock.

The time had come for doggy training classes, said the vet, so that Sally would know exactly who the master was in our house. I couldn't recall having to take any classes to get that idea across to my children, but $100 for a good night's sleep seemed reasonable, so off we went. By the end of the month-long course, she had learned to sit, as long as she really felt like sitting. As an added bonus, she learned how to jump up and ruin favorite sweaters. And though we tried tons of suggestions, we were still battling the wake-up-call barking problem.

One day I found an anonymous letter in the mailbox. A concerned neighbor thought that Sally might need more attention. Perhaps she's barking so we'll spend more time with her. At six in the morning. They were only thinking of the poor, "neglected" dog; the "incessant barking" wasn't bothering them at all. But could we possibly do something?

We (okay, mostly me) decided Sally needed a home in the country with enough space to bark her fool head off without bothering buttinski neighbors. She needed someone like a hunter, who understood an active breed like Sally. An ad was put in the paper: *Pointer/Beagle. Free to a good home.* The dog had been de-wormed, vaccinated, spayed, and trained (sort of), and came with her own crate. Yessir, Sally was a real bargain.

The phone rang a week later while my husband was in the shower. A bachelor, living in a rural area, needed a hunting dog and loved pointers. Was Sally still available? Until then, every caller had been deterred by Sally's "rambunctious nature." But this guy had definite potential.

I shouted to my husband over the rushing water.

"Someone wants Sally. He lives way out in the country."

"Okay," yelled my husband.

"He doesn't have kids, so the jumping won't be a problem."

"Okay," he yelled again.

I stood outside the shower. A minute passed.

"Well, what now?" asked my husband, suds running down his back.

It seemed ideal. Except now I was sniffling outside the shower door. "I don't think I can give Sally away."

"Oh, for heaven's sake," said my husband.

Sally had outlasted me. We purchased baby gates to enclose the kitchen, Sally's domain for the evening and early morning hours. Her new, larger crate took up half the dining area. Sally was still a yard dog during most of the day, but she often managed to escape. She'd run around the house in a blur, ending up on the front porch, waiting for someone to bring her inside. So much for the fence.

But Sally had more tricks up her doggy sleeves. Now she barked all day. She barked at the neighbor mowing the lawn. She barked at the kids getting off the bus. She barked at lizards, squirrels, and shadows. When her barking reached a crescendo, we'd give a call and up the stairs bolted Sally. She was so happy to be inside she'd jump on anyone within catapulting distance. Clearly, Sally had all the signs of a raging juvenile delinquent. It was time for something drastic. Something known as doggy boot camp.

Every day the boot camp instructor would call with a glowing report of Sally's progress. We had always known Sally was smarter than she looked, so we weren't at all surprised. If Sally had to be perfectly trained before she could come home, then Sally would go to the head of the class in record time. By week's end, we excitedly returned for our wonder dog.

But first we had to master all the commands and prove our expertise as trainers. Our chests swelled with pride as Sally "heeled" like a pro. Our throats choked with emotion while she "sat" like a statue. Our jaws dropped when she "stayed" in the same spot for at least five minutes. It was a miracle!

A miracle! And it had cost us only $500. We left boot camp with our new and improved Sally dog and a training video. . . .

And we pulled into our driveway with the same old Sally, barking like a maniac as she sprang from the smelly car.

John's old enough to drive now, so that makes Sally pretty old too. She still barks at anything and anybody, but nobody really notices much anymore. She's still racking up expenses, but the budget has expanded along with her girth. The only time she's ever in the yard these days is when John is in the yard too, right beside her. Heck, we don't even bother with the gates unless a service person is around. But not because Sally jumps. She never jumps on anyone. She did learn that lesson. I guess we finally learned something too.

One fine spring day we got a dog and named her Sally. Sally Hall. And this is her home, always. Because family is for keeps, no matter what the cost.

~Cathy C. Hall

Born to Be Wild

"M om!" My son Ben stomped up the stairs from where he'd been playing outside with his younger siblings, Chloe and Sam. The anxiety in his steps was the kind a mom hates to hear; it usually means someone is bleeding. "Sam let Dakota out of the yard, and she's gone!" he said, gasping to catch his breath.

It took most of my strength to contain the expletives that leapt to mind. It was hardly the first time this had happened, and Sam wasn't the only perpetrator. I'd done it, my husband had done it, and every child except the toddler had done it at least once.

"You go make sure the gate is closed before Kelly gets out, and I'll go get Dakota," I told him.

I headed out the front door and immediately spotted Dakota in the cul de sac. I called to her, but when she looked at me, I heard the lyrics of "Born to Be Wild" in my head. Dakota had a penchant for heading down the roadway in search of adventure. As I stepped toward her, she bounded down the street, stopping only to see how close I was.

I called down curses on her head and followed her at a slow walk. If I ran, she would run faster. If I acted desperate to catch her, it would only make her more elusive. If I called more than a few times, she'd just hide and play tag with me. We'd done this before. It was her one failing: Give her an open gate, and she would run.

I called her name a few times. A neighbor looked up from spraying weeds in his sidewalk. "She's a good listener, huh?" he chuckled.

"Oh yeah, she's brilliant," I said. Dakota, meanwhile, kept running.

When I got to the end of the cul de sac, I turned around. The choice had to be made—chase a dog who didn't want to be caught but would probably come back anyway, or go make sure my seven-, five-, and three-year-old children didn't do something else I'd have to fix. It wasn't a tough choice.

It had never been a tough choice, to be honest. Like many people who have dogs before kids, we'd seen our dog take a back seat to each successive baby.

Dakota pre-dated our kids by about three-and-a-half years. She'd been our baby before we had babies. We got her about six months after finally buying our first home. We'd had cats for a couple of years by that point, and I would have been happy with just the cats for quite a while. Much as I love dogs, I was content. My husband, though, wanted a dog now that we had a yard, and since he put up with my cats, who was I to argue?

We brought Dakota home when she was about six weeks old. A black Lab/German shepherd mix, she was small enough to fit in my cupped hands. She was a snuggler; we could tip her back and cradle her like a baby, and she would fall asleep. She was so small at first that when we tried to get her to jump up our backdoor step, she would just sit at the bottom, barking at us and wiggling her hindquarters as if to say, "You gotta know, Mom, I'd do it if I could!"

As soon as she was housetrained, we started letting her sleep on our bed. She was a warm little lump between us that grew until we had to start pushing her to the end of the bed. Fortunately, she stopped growing at about forty-five pounds. She slept on our bed for a couple of years, and we became kindred spirits in our opinion of alarm clocks. When mine went off at 5:30 every morning, Dakota would groan, stretch, and bury her head. "I agree," I told her every morning. Dutifully, she'd hop down when I got up, and I'd put her in the yard for the day. In the evenings, she'd come in and sit on the couch with us and watch TV or sit on the floor in front of us with our feet rubbing her belly. We were a threesome. A family.

Babies were inevitable, though. I became pregnant with our first child, Ben, in October 1998. For a while, Dakota held her place in the bed, but as my belly grew and I battled nausea and insomnia, she ended up pushed to the floor. She still had her blanket and still groaned every morning, but I just couldn't share the bed with her.

When the baby came, we moved Dakota to the hall outside our bedroom door at night. If she groaned when the alarm went off, I reasoned, how much more would she complain with a crying baby? Besides, since I had quit my job to stay home with the baby, Dakota would have more time with me and the baby during the day.

For a while, it worked well that way. Dakota was enamored with Ben from the start. I'm convinced she knew he was part of me and his dad. She never saw him as an interloper. When he started crawling, I'd hover and watch carefully, not fully trusting her, since she'd never been around babies. She never even came close to giving me cause for alarm. She let Ben crawl all over her, tail wagging the whole time. It was like she had finally become a mommy too.

Things were cruising along until December of 2000. I was pregnant with baby number two and already feeling crowded in the house with a toddler, a dog, three cats, and a growing belly. My mom called one night and said someone had dumped a young puppy on her, and she couldn't keep the little thing. Would we be interested in a companion for Dakota? The pup was a black Lab, about five months old, and very sweet. We took her, and Dakota was thrilled. "A puppy of my very own!" her brown eyes sang. "Now I am a mom!"

But two dogs in a house already bursting at the seams? No. I had to insist—they'd be outside most of the time. They slept in the living room at night until the puppy, Kelly, damaged the couches and toys one too many times. Then we put them in the utility room at night. I'm sure Dakota must have thought, "Ah, how the mighty have fallen!"

Since then, Dakota has seen a lot of changes—a move, three more babies, the loss of one cat. She's happy and adaptable; she's wonderful with the kids' and we all adore her. But still, give her an open gate, and she will run every time.

I'm convinced it's not because she's unhappy here. I watch her with the kids, and I can see pure dog love in her eyes. She adores them. When they are leading her around by the collar and feeding her fruit from our backyard, she's in heaven. I've felt guilty in the past for not paying enough attention to her, but then, the kids do that, and she was made for them.

I think that, for Dakota, it's the lure of the open road that she just can't resist. Somewhere, under all of the adoration and love of her family, she's a wild dog. She wants to explore. It doesn't matter if she's smelled the same smells a hundred times, it's all new every time. There's freedom in her eyes when she heads off down the street. She loves her home, and she will come back—but only after she's smelled some smells, tasted some tastes, and heard some noises.

Dakota is ten years old now. She hobbles a little on cold mornings. There's more gray than black in her beard. Her teeth are starting to show some wear. But in her eyes, there's still a spark of intelligence and a desire for new experiences. Couldn't we all use some of that in our dotage?

When I got back to the house, I scolded the kids for letting her out of the gate and made them stay in the house.

"Will Dakota come back?" Ben asked.

"I don't know," I answered honestly. "Probably.

But she's old, and she likes to run. You just never know."

About half an hour later, I heard a familiar jingle. Dakota was padding down the street, stopping every few feet to smell something. I grabbed a half cup of dog food and went out to lure her in. It still took several minutes of coaxing to get her back, but once I did, she ran in the house and straight downstairs to the chorus of three voices shouting, "Dakota!" She reveled in the adoration and then asked to go back out in the backyard. I'm sure she had an adventure to tell Kelly.

Later in the day I noticed her sleeping soundly in one of the deck chairs, probably done in by her adventure. There was a look of smug satisfaction on her face, though. I think Dakota has become one of those red hat ladies you hear about, the ones who wear red and purple and don't care what other people think. Dakota doesn't care what I think about her wanderings. She doesn't care if it's inconvenient to me. She just wants to have an adventure.

As for me, I'm glad the old girl is back. Even though she's sometimes inconvenient, she's family.

~Amy Rose Davis

Sandy Dreams

S andy is a fourteen-year-old, twenty-two-pound canine angel of dubious pedigree. With the tail of a beagle, the body of a stunted greyhound, and ears like Yoda, "beautiful" is a term never used to describe her. As further proof, please watch the movie *Ice Age* and take a good look at Skrat, a character some have said looks suspiciously like Sandy's litter mate.

Although I acknowledge Sandy's interesting features, I don't see her mismatched body parts and cartoon expressions. I see her soft, pale fur and soulful, amber eyes surrounded by lovely, thick, white lashes. Those tender eyes have, over the course of many years, regarded me with surprise, excitement, sympathy, devotion, and always, love—deep, true, unconditional love.

I recently learned that Sandy is in the early stages of kidney failure. This is not a surprising diagnosis for a dog of her advanced years. The veterinarian spoke with me at length about the efforts we can make to keep her comfortable and reasonably content in the short time she has left. Eventually, our family will have to decide whether Sandy should be euthanized. This is a decision I have never had to make for a pet, and I am not looking forward to it now.

Earlier today, I was feeling sorry for us both, and Sandy did something she never fails to do when I'm down. She cheered me up. It was quite unintentional on her part, as she was sound asleep at the time, yet it was symbolic of the joy and comfort she has always provided.

I was sitting in my office when I heard Sandy yip. She rarely barks anymore, her hearing having been stolen by age, so it was an unexpected sound. I glanced at her and smiled. Of course, she was dreaming. Her legs were aquiver, and her small feet scratched at the carpet. *Yip!* She made the sound again, eyes closed, body parts vibrating as if she were trying to run. *Yip! Yip!* How could I not smile?

I spent the better part of ten minutes imagining what she might be dreaming. Not chasing squirrels. Though she used to bark "hello" to them, she was too gentle in nature to run them off. Perhaps she was chasing a tennis ball. Or maybe she was dreaming of her dearest canine buddy, Riley, our beloved golden retriever, possessed with boatloads of charm and very little brain. Older than Sandy, Riley died several years ago. Sandy's decline began shortly thereafter. The interaction between the two dogs was indicative of Sandy's innate kindness and gentle spirit.

Riley was a good old boy, a tad overweight, and just beginning to suffer from arthritis. Still, he was a retriever, and true to his breed, retrieving was one of the things Riley loved best. Sandy was quite a bit younger than Riley and certainly faster and more agile than he had ever been, even in his puppy years. She, too, loved to chase and retrieve tennis balls, an activity she could easily have pursued all day. Riley had to work hard to beat her to the ball, but it was a race they both enjoyed.

One day we were in the backyard playing fetch. I'd throw the ball to the very edge of the yard, and before poor old, arthritic Riley was even halfway there, Sandy would scoop up the ball and be on her way back to me. After two or three rounds of this, though, something incredible happened. Sandy stopped bringing me the ball. Oh, she couldn't stop herself from taking chase as soon as I let the fuzzy green thing fly. She sped past Riley to the fence, captured the ball, and trotted halfway up the yard to her old golden friend. Then she dropped the ball in front of him and ran off, allowing him the honor of picking up the prize and delivering it back to me.

Never once after that day did she bring me the ball. Until the day Riley died, Sandy delivered the ball to her aging buddy so he could enjoy the game too.

While on vacation several years ago, we boarded our pets with the veterinarian. We always kenneled the dogs together, because they were such good friends and because Sandy, who could be a bit high strung at times, was always happier and calmer when rooming with her pal. During our absence, Riley became seriously ill. The vet told us later that Sandy curled up next to Riley and never left his side. She had been his companion for fun and games, and she offered what comfort she could in his death.

Yip! Yip! Yip!

I smiled again, watching Sandy, still dreaming, as my ruminations continued. . . .

Sandy jumping into our car—uninvited—on the day we met her, so certain we were the right family for her. Smart dog.

Sandy, our escape artist, digging holes under the fence and then, much to our dismay, actually climbing up and over the fence with the agility of a chimpanzee.

Sandy, our fierce protector, barking often and loudly at anything she perceived as a threat, whether it be a person, a stray dog, or a piece of newspaper blown into the yard.

Yip! Yip! Yip!

I glanced at the clock, realized I was losing the afternoon. Still, it was time well spent. My sadness had dissipated, and my heart and mind were left with the realization that Sandy would always be with us, just as Riley was. Thoughts of Sandy had brought Riley back to me today, another of Sandy's unwitting gifts.

Despite the ravages of age or the sorrow that will eventually come, the important thing is that the old girl is still with us. There are a few months of love yet to share with Sandy. When the time comes for her to leave us, I know she will be in good paws with her best pal, Riley. He is undoubtedly sitting at the edge of some heavenly meadow, tongue lolling, green tennis ball at his feet, watching and waiting for the arrival of his dearest friend. I wouldn't be surprised if he brings her the ball next time.

~Lisa Ricard Claro

Hope in a Dumpster

I was thirty years old when I met Dumpster, a sixty-pound, black-and-tan mutt, wandering through the alley in back of my 1930s apartment building in the Capitol Hill area of central Denver. I had seen him around the trash bins for about a week and figured he must have been dumped there. He was a little scary-looking—unkempt, with intense and vigilant eyes—and I wasn't used to being around dogs. But I wasn't afraid.

I called him over and was immediately overtaken by long-dormant maternal instincts. He approached me tentatively, tucking his tail between his legs, his head bowed down, unable or unwilling to meet my eyes. Oh, he was brave, but also gentle and regal and so like the dog of my childhood dreams, the one I'd longed for and never had.

My one and only girlhood desire was not the

standard owning-a-horse wish; I wanted a dog—more then anything on God's earth. I spent hours poring over books about the various breeds and how to raise and train a puppy. I practiced with my stuffed animals and made lists of suitable dog names. It was a modest dream for a middle-class girl in the 1970s. But my mother, an extreme germ-o-phobic, declared animals dirty and disease-ridden and would not have such a beast in her house.

From the time I was eight or nine until I hit thirteen, I left hundreds of notes proclaiming my desperation in my mom's underwear drawers: "I want a dog." "My life is not complete without a dog." "Please get me a dog." It was all for naught. Although my dad was not at all opposed to the idea, Mom was the boss and she refused to budge.

With adolescence, my attention turned to more essential endeavors, leaving no room to dream about dogs. Instead, I spent my time worrying about how my hair looked, whether the guy in math class noticed my new high-fashion multi-colored toe socks, and if I would ever get to see the movie *Saturday Night Fever*.

After high school and college and graduate school, I settled into the life of a working single woman, coming home to an empty apartment, where I'd fix a frozen dinner and dream of meeting Mr. Right. By the time I reached thirty, I had all but forgotten about my dream of having my own dog. I had long ago accepted that life was unfair, that things didn't always turn out the way I wanted them to, and that dreams were necessary only to create some kind of hope. Without hope, life could be unbearably tedious. Now, I dreamed of owning a house, where I wouldn't have to put up with the idiosyncrasies of too-close neighbors. But like the dog dream, I knew it would never happen. I was a social worker in a city of accountants and engineers; I could not afford the luxury of my own home. So I satisfied myself with what I had, and it was a good life, as far as it went. . . .

Until I met *him*.

For a few days, I left out food for Dumpster, bought him bones to chew, and laid a blanket under the lone tree in the urban alley where he slept. I hoped that someone else would rescue him, take him to a real home, and treat him like the king he so obviously was. I could not keep him in my apartment—no pets allowed.

I realized this was no life for a dog, alone and wandering without a pack in the concrete jungle. After calling several shelters, I found one that promised me he would not be put to sleep, even if they could find no home for him. When the new caretakers informed me that he was a she, Dumpster's regal bearing transformed into sophisticated beauty before my very eyes. She would be safe now; I had done a good thing. With some tears, I let her go.

The foster home parents assigned by the animal shelter named her Eve, which didn't quite fit. But I had no say in the matter; she was no longer "my" dog. I visited her at her new temporary home, brought her toys and treats, and took her on long walks. Slowly, it dawned on me. This *was* my dog. I may have given up on my dream, but it had not given up on me.

I set about finding a home for Eve-Dumpster and me. Eve-Dumpster. E D. That was it! I renamed her Edie.

Over the next two months, I must have called fifty apartments—none of which would accept dogs—and another twenty rental homes, trying to find a place for us. Then I looked for a home to buy, spending all my free time traipsing through less-than-adequate dwellings. It seemed that in my price range, "house" meant either "ugly, cramped, yard-less condominium" or "dilapidated hut in a scary neighborhood."

I was losing hope. Maybe dreams were meant to be just dreams and nothing more. But I wanted this dog so badly. After all, I was the one who had rescued her from a life on the streets or possibly worse. It didn't seem right that someone else could adopt and keep her for all time. But the foster home let me know that would soon happen; my time was running out.

I made one last phone call. When the man on the other end of the line told me he had just rented out his house to someone else, I broke down in tears and told him my story. I needed a house now, or I would lose the chance to adopt my dog.

Not only was this man a dog-lover, but he also had a friend who was readying a small home to put on the market. I called the friend and went to look at the house. It was perfect: just the right size, with a large fenced yard and an extra bedroom for the dog accessories. It was only two miles from my apartment. Miraculously, he named a price within my reach.

And so Edie became my dog, and that perfect, tiny house became our home. I used to joke that I had bought her the biggest dog house the world had ever known. That is probably true. But it's also true that she brought me home to that place inside where hopes and dreams aren't just distractions from everyday life.

Edie was my dream, and she also made my dreams come true. She gave me hope. After all, if that demure lady could survive being dumped in an alley alone, face each day with hope and courage, and not run away when approached by a stranger, surely I could find a way to give her, to give us, a home. Even on my meager salary, in a city of accountants and engineers.

Over the years, I've told this story to many people and received numerous accolades for adopting a castaway mutt rather than a purebred with papers. What they don't quite understand is that I didn't rescue Edie. She rescued me.

~Sue Dallman-Carrizales

Doggie Do-Si-Do

She started drinking, you know, after all the kids left for college," a friend whispered to me about a woman whose husband had just left her. "It happens more often than you think." She looked knowingly at me. Was she looking at me that way because she knew I would never do that or because she feared I would?

I have to admit, I was a tad worried about how I would fill my life after the last chick left the nest. There was my writing, of course, but I'd been doing that all along. How would I fill those hours that had previously been spent volunteering at school and driving carpools? And how would I fill that ache in my heart? I love being with my children and their friends. Having a house full of kids watching TV and eating everything in my pantry was my idea of a fun evening.

Visions of liquor bottles strewn around the house drove me to sign up for volunteer work as my youngest child prepared to depart for college. Working with children eased the pain as he drove off that fall, but I knew it wasn't enough. I wrote more and busied myself with redecorating the house, but I still missed my kids and their friends.

"You have got to do something about this dog," my husband scolded one evening, as Duchess raced around the living room, toppling furniture and terrorizing the cat. We'd adopted Duchess, an Australian cattle dog, from animal control when she was an eight-month-old, skinny, scared pup who cowered any time someone spoke in a raised voice. Food and love had cured those problems, only to be replaced by new ones. Cattle dogs are bred to chase cows in the Australian outback for hours at a time. They can outrun the Energizer Bunny and hardly be out of breath.

Duchess's obedience instructor had suggested she do agility training, where dogs climb, jump, and maneuver obstacles as fast as they can on a course. I'd dismissed the idea when I still had one child at home because I didn't have time, but my newly empty nest suddenly provided me with plenty of free hours. So one evening I loaded Duchess in the car, along with a water bowl (she refused to drink from the one provided in class) and a bag full of treats for her first try at agility training.

Within a few months, she was jumping, tearing through tunnels, racing over the A-frame, and winding her way through the weave poles. Even my husband began coming to class and cheering her on, which made her try all the harder. He became our coach, discussing strategies for running the course and suggesting ways I could improve my handling.

Then at dinner one night, we enlightened a group of friends about the intricacies and challenges of agility training, proudly pointing to our now well-behaved and quiet dog. Duchess would look up whenever anyone mentioned her name, but didn't beg for food or bother any of our guests. I was just beginning to explain how to train a dog to maneuver the weave poles, when our friend Marci cleared her throat and pushed back her chair.

"You know," she said, "I'm going to come over here one day and that dog's going to be in a soccer uniform."

I laughed along with the rest of the group, but knew in my heart that none of them "got it."

Duchess won her first ribbon, a third place, at a meet just before Thanksgiving. With family and friends gathered around the table, I passed photos of her clearing a jump with plenty of room to spare and made everyone look at the huge, yellow ribbon.

"You seriously need some grandkids," one cousin suggested as she passed the ribbon along.

"I don't need grandkids," I responded. "I have Duchess." I saw her roll her eyes, but pretended not to notice.

At Christmas, my husband got a cap with a cattle dog embroidered on it, so he could look official as he coached us. I got a bag to carry our equipment to the meets and an apron with a cattle dog on it. They were our favorite presents.

Disaster struck one evening in class when Duchess refused to jump or climb. I took her immediately to the vet the next morning, and X-rays revealed that an old injury was acting up.

"She's only four," the vet mumbled as he studied the calcium deposits along her spine. "I think she was injured before you adopted her; she might have been kicked or hit there." Rest and medication would heal her for now, but he warned us that agility work would probably be too tough for her in another year or two.

The three of us moped around the house for several weeks as the inflammation in her back slowly disappeared. Every Thursday evening, she would stand expectantly by the door, waiting for me to take her to class. My husband's new cap hung uselessly in the closet.

Just when life had begun to feel like a drag for all three of us, a woman we knew from agility class called. "I know Duchess is on hiatus from agility," she said. "We're starting a doggie square dance group, and we'd like to invite you and Duchess to join us."

I immediately called my husband at work and gave him the good news.

"You aren't seriously considering this?" he questioned. "Doggie square dancing?"

I scolded him for his lack of enthusiasm, reminding him that we'd been invited to join this elite group. I explained that it was simply obedience moves set to music and that it would provide good exercise for Duchess without putting strain on her injury. Then I informed him that we would be performing in six weeks in the home show at the convention center, demonstrating basic obedience skills in dance movements with a real square dance caller. We would represent the training center. Plus, we were going to be on local television.

"I'm going to have to see this to believe it," he sighed.

"I am seriously worried about you," my brother said the next day on the phone. "Doggie square dancing?"

I again explained, as I had to my husband, how it was really obedience moves set to music, that we were a demonstration team, and that Duchess needed something to do until her back healed. He didn't seem convinced.

Ten of us were on the team, but only eight would perform at the home show, so Duchess and I practiced every day to make sure we made the cut. We did, and for three days, she heeled, sat, stayed, and danced her way into the hearts of the audience. As we strolled through the home show on the last day, my husband insisted on holding her leash as people stopped to pet her and ask questions.

That evening, as the three of us collapsed on the couch, the phone rang. "Would you like to meet for a drink?" some friends asked.

"No thanks," we told them. "We're dog-tired."

So much for the dreaded humdrums of an empty nest. Something told me we were going to be just fine—my husband, my dancing partner, and I.

~Susan Luzader

Dogs Who Do Things

My father was a sportswriter. While his profession had many influences on our family, perhaps its biggest impact has been on the dozen or so dogs who have come and gone in my life. This is most evident in their names.

My first dog was Saratoga Roach, a determined little beagle named for the summer racetrack in upstate New York. Later there was Cleveland, a hapless chocolate Lab named after the Browns. For years I have looked for a dog to name Pete, for Pistol Pete Maravich, the late basketball-scoring champ. My dog Pete would have to be medium-sized, with a shingle of hair that bounced over his eyes and the gift to leap, catch, and retrieve until the day he died.

But being a dog in a sportswriter's family attracts more subtle influences than a name. Perhaps even more than the human progeny of the writer, our dogs were measured by the sports they chose *not* to play. Two of my father's friends were Nelson Bryant, the legendary field-and-stream reporter, and Red Smith, who wrote near poetry under a sports byline. Over the years, Mr. Bryant complained bitterly to both Mr. Smith and Mr. Roach about their dogs. While his dogs could hunt, ours, it seemed, didn't "do" anything.

By Mr. Bryant's standards, I can say with great certainty that I have never lived with a dog who could do anything. That is not to say I've never known any dogs who could do things to fascinate, delight, or educate the people who live with them. Friends of mine in Cambridge had a dog who regularly rode the Boston MBTA alone with great élan. And I once knew a dog named Homely who retrieved quarters thrown over a barn and into the woods.

Cleveland, my Labrador, could retrieve. While it's true that he never brought me a bird I wanted to eat, he did keep me flush with golf balls, stealing jaws-full off the back nine we lived on in New York's Adirondack Mountains. The minute a ball whomped against the house, he'd slam through the screen door with a gusto that would have made Pavlov proud. More than once I rescued him from a threatening nine iron waved above the head of a golfer. Clevie would romp like a demented caddie after a birdie, his great mouth stuffed with the balls off several greens. In his prime, he could hold four, though I don't pretend to think that's what's meant by the term "sporting breed."

In the period between Cleveland and my next canine, I met a man who had never lived with a dog. Neither had his father nor his father before him. So I married the man and set about to change all that.

Softening his resolve began by auditioning names for the incipient dog. After a few weeks, the options narrowed to bird breeds, the logic being that for a honeymoon period, anyway, my new spouse deserved to believe that his dog might actually do something. Much as expectant parents mouth children's names, I would call them out to no one in particular. Then one summer afternoon I looked up from my gardening to see a filthy, yellow and white, plume-tailed, young dog trot into our yard. She was wearing a red ribbon around her neck.

"Mallard!" I yelled, dropping my trowel.

"Oh, no," my husband replied into the topsoil.

She loped right up to me and licked my face. Mallard was with us for two unsteady years, during which time she would occasionally walk out of the yard just as unabashedly as she had walked in, staying away for weeks. She always returned with a red ribbon tied neatly around her neck, and was never with us on holidays. So we figured we shared her with someone and were grateful for the time she chose to spend with us. After all, her affection for us was lavish. She sat primly in the canoe for paddles of any duration and never ran away from anywhere but home.

One day she left and didn't return. We never knew why. But my husband has a penchant for telling anyone who will listen that if I hadn't renamed her for a migrating bird, she would not have taken to behaving like one. For a while, he would have also told you that the only thing dogs do is break your heart.

We waited, dogless, for a year, before we got a call from a friend in Mexico whose aunt had just died, leaving behind her three-year-old Weimaraner. If the family paid the transit, our friend wanted to know, would we accept the dog into our home? Of course.

Her name was Coqueta, Coca for short. European-bred, this dog was the biggest Weimaraner I had ever seen. She weighed in at eighty pounds and stood tall enough to fall asleep with her head on the dining room table. And, amazingly, she did things. Unfortunately, she understood commands only in Spanish. This proved humiliating during obedience school, when all around were mutts of eager discipline while we awaited the response of a fancy dog laid flat on the floor as we pleaded urgently for her to sit up.

Coca had been raised in a walled garden, the precious companion of a well-to-do eccentric woman. Initially, that limited the things she wanted to do in any language. She'd sit near the fireplace, her paws crossed below her breast, and look at us in a purebred Katharine Hepburn demeanor, as if waiting for the conversation to become engaging enough for her to participate. My husband's theory was that no one had ever asked her to do anything. He may have been right, because during our nine years together, she did learn to run all day beside a cross-country skier, climb the high peaks of the Adirondacks, and selflessly listen to the world of problems that this woman regularly emptied into her vast heart.

When we became parents, Coca, like many nannies before her, rose to the new occasion and ballooned to nearly 100 pounds, sitting pretty under the high chair's continuous stream of flotsam and jetsam. Outside, she guarded the playpen with her great head over demurely folded paws, snapping her jaws at flies that threatened to attack the sweet-smelling child napping in the shade.

All too soon it seemed that everyone in our household was either male or young, except me and Coca. We started going for slower walks, bonded

in a war against aging, or at least it seemed so to
me. Then we went less frequently, and then I merely
looked in on her when I went walking alone. Then
I carried her outside—the dwindling seventy pounds
of her sustaining dignity. Then, toward the end,
I just let her be and cleaned up after her. Eventually, despite my best efforts, it was too much for her,
so I took her to the vet, the last appointment of the
day, and cradled her against my heart as she died.

I loved that dog more than I love most of my
friends, and I am not ashamed to say that I also
found her more intelligent than some. It seems to
me that while I rarely meet a dog I do not like, I frequently come across people I cannot bear.

But I am an easy mark. The real test was my husband, whose loss I thought I'd have to look hard to
see. Then I remembered that Coca did a little dance
every night when he walked through the door, and
that once or twice I had caught him doing it right
along with her. He had bought her the orange T-
shirt in hunting season, so no one would mistake her
for a deer. And there is that snapshot of them napping together, her paw resting on his shoulder. I realized that what Coca did best was reach my husband
in ways that Mallard never could, teaching him that
dogs are good to the end and that, even after death,
they can remain steadfast parts of what we are proud

to call home. Coca did what all dogs can do, if we don't mess with them too much: She converted him to a person who can love almost any dog.

That is a good thing, since we now live with a dog with dark problems only love can reach.

Our German shorthaired pointer came to us with his name, which is Chase. It's a fitting name, I guess, since it is in his nature is to do such things. But then nurture intervened. A rescue dog, Chase arrived at our house at a year-and-a-half, miserably thin, and recovering from a broken pelvis and a fractured leg come by unnaturally from the cruel hands of his former owners. How this dog could like anyone, I will never know. The first night he fell asleep bolt upright, with his head stuffed under the covers on my side of the bed. He would awaken as he fell over, only to right himself, shove his great nose back between the mattress and the sheets, and fall asleep again, breathing into the backs of my knees. It was weeks before I could coax him into his own bed.

Chase spends virtually every moment next to me: on my feet when I type, between the legs of my chair when I eat, at the bus stop waiting for our daughter to come home from school so he can climb the ladder with us to her playhouse. It's really only tough in the shower. As soon as I go in and turn on the jet, the shower curtain will be tossed open by a

long, brown nose. There will be Chase, all eighty-
five muscled pounds of him, his head thrust full into
the steam, his eyes squinting amid the spray and
falling lather. When I take a bath, his massive neck
and head hover over the tub as he vigilantly licks my
knees clean of any offending bubbles.

Somewhere in his great soul, I think, he's urgently
trying to work off whatever vast unknown sin he
might have committed that got him beaten so sav-
agely and begging me to love him. But, of course, he
doesn't have to do that: I was his the minute we met.
After all, it's been a long time since I was the on this
end of the mute adoration of a teenage boy. There
is little in its slavish version of devotion that doesn't
improve a woman.

He does other things as well: He can whistle
through his nose, catch flies while bouncing and
pivoting on his hind legs, and dig trenches for my
daffodil bulbs. And he listens keenly for the word
"kennel"—or any word that sounds similar—which
cues him to exit to that place where he feels most
safe.

But perhaps what Chase does best is share the
burden he feels. At night, he goes up to the bedroom when I do, and as I read he sits nearby. Only
when my husband finally comes up and is settled
in bed will Chase amble down the stairs to his ken-

nel—assured, it seems, that I am well protected and he can get some rest.

Actually, I rarely call him Chase. Early on I gave him nicknames—from Honeyman to Chowderhead—that are not the sort of sports sobriquets that run in my family. This dog is just not the sporting type. All efforts to get him to work like his breed make him roll onto his back and beg off. What he does, though, is carry a penchant for love that not even a human being could beat out of him. And while sometimes I wonder if calling him Chase would get him to do more traditional things, I think he's doing enough.

~Marion Roach

Beauty in the Beast

One of my grandmother's favorite expressions was "You can't judge a book by its cover." I never fully understood its meaning until my husband and I started our search for a family dog.

We had just purchased our first home, and for the first time we could have pets larger than a hamster. I was considering a cat, but my husband had grown up with dogs and wanted our children to experience the same joys of canine companionship that he had cherished during his childhood. But finding the right dog for our family ended up being anything but a joy. We spent countless hours looking at puppies and even brought a few home on a trial basis, but none of them seemed to be a good fit with our family. I gave up, declared our lifestyle unsuitable for a dog, and moved on.

But my husband refused to abandon hope. He missed having a dog around and remained certain that our perfect dog was out there somewhere, just waiting for us. He called the Humane Society and left his name, asking them to call if they received any mature large dogs, especially German shepherds. His logic was that an older dog would have a well-established clear personality, and it would be easier to see whether the dog's personality fit with us. Two days later, the Humane Society called about someone who desperately needed to get rid of their shepherd.

"Great," I said. "When will they be bringing the dog to the shelter?"

There was a long pause on the other end of the line. "He's not going to drop the dog off here. You'll have to go to his house to see it."

I thought that was a little odd, but took down the man's number anyway and called him to set up a visit. The mystery was solved when we arrived at his house.

When we pulled up his driveway, a red Sasquatch began throwing itself against the closed garage door. The dog was huge, at least ninety pounds, with long, bushy hair that stuck out in every direction. It was frothing at the mouth and barking loud enough to make my teeth hurt. The garage windows were smeared with angry foam.

We stayed in the car while the garage door went up.

"It's okay, she's on her leash," her owner yelled. He waved for us to come into the garage as he called the dog back to his side. She came and obediently sat down beside him, watching us suspiciously as we got out of the car, dropping her ear-splitting barks to low huffs and growls.

"This is Natasha," the man said.

"Hi, Natasha," I said hesitantly.

That set her off barking again, but she didn't move from the man's side.

I took a good look at her: long gold and red fur, feathery plumes from the backs of her legs, sharp snout, golden eyes. The thick ruff of gold and red fur framing her face made her look lionesque. I decided she looked like a cross between a Kodiak bear and an African lion.

While we talked to the man, the dog watched us suspiciously. I tried to approach her a few times, but each time she warned me back.

Eventually the man said, "So what do you think?"

"She's the most beautiful dog I've ever seen. But she seems pretty aggressive," I said.

He chuckled and stroked her head. "She's not really aggressive. She's just protective. Right now her job is to protect me, but if you take her home, her new job will be to protect you."

As if to prove it, Natasha let her tongue loll out of the side of her mouth and looked up at her owner adoringly.

"I don't know how we'd even get her home," I said. In truth, I was just making excuses; I had already given up on her. Obviously, she had aggression issues. The whole time we'd been there, neither my husband nor I had been able to get close to her. Her owner could give me reassurances until the cows came home, but it wouldn't change my mind. Maybe she was "just protective," but what if she weren't? What if she was just plain old mean? Yet something in me wanted to bring her home. Maybe it was because I knew the owner's chances of finding a home for her were slim. Surely other people would have the same reaction I'd had. I was torn between wanting to save her from being put to sleep and wanting to save myself from the risk of a killer dog.

The man patted her on the head. When he spoke, his voice was thick. "We love her to death, but we've got to move. We can't afford the house anymore, and our new apartment won't let us keep her."

He reached down and unclipped Natasha's leash. Then he hurried over to my van and threw open the door. "Time to go bye-bye, Natasha," he said.

She sprung up, trotted right past me—while I stood frozen, too frightened to even breathe—and hopped into our van. She went straight to the back and laid down across the back seat. I looked at my husband. His eyes were as wide as mine felt.

I opened my mouth to protest, but before I could get a word out, the man slammed the van door shut and handed me a big bag of dog biscuits. "She loves these," he said. Then he turned and walked back into his house, never once looking back.

My husband and I stood in silent shock for a moment, and in his eyes I could see the same thing I was thinking: "What now?"

I walked over to the van and peeked in. Natasha was lying across the back seat—the whole back seat—watching the garage for the man to reappear. My husband and I opened our doors slowly, ready to abandon the van if Natasha moved. She didn't. We cautiously slid in, leaving our legs still hanging out, ready to run. Natasha didn't make a sound. When my husband started the van, she sat up and looked out the window.

"Do you think I should go get him and make him get his dog?" he asked me. I could see he was torn too.

I looked back at Natasha, sitting across the back seat. "Well, let's drive around for a few minutes and see what she does. If she starts to freak out, we'll bring her back."

As we drove around town, Natasha just sat in the back peacefully, staring out the window, her tongue lolling.

"Well," my husband finally asked, on our fourth trip around the small town, "what do we do now?"

"Let's go home, I guess."

Halfway through the hour-long drive home, Natasha poked her head between the two front seats. My husband and I both stiffened. She turned to look at him, turned the other way to look at me, sighed, and went back to lie down in the backseat.

We arrived home late, well after our children's bedtime, which I was thankful for. I didn't want them anywhere near the wildcard dog until I figured out what her true nature was. I let her out of the van, and she padded past me, into the house (without so much as a bark or growl), and right into the living room . . . where my children were all asleep on the floor! I panicked. But Natasha went and stood over them and licked them all awake, her huge tail whisking up a hurricane. The kids immediately threw their arms around her neck and buried her in bear hugs. Natasha just sat and grinned. Those golden eyes that had been full of anger and suspicion earlier now sparkled with joy.

A few weeks later, my neighbor had her daycare kids out in her yard when I brought Natasha out for a potty break. The daycare kids rushed to the fence and poked their hands through, asking to "pet the bear." By that time, I knew Natasha wasn't a vicious dog, so I brought her over to meet them. She immediately turned broadside to the fence and leaned in, so that there was room for all the little hands to pet every inch of her, from head to tail. They petted her and poked her and prodded her—all the while, her tongue lolled out in grin and her eyes were half-closed in ecstasy, loving every minute of it.

She was eighteen months old when we brought her home. She's nine now, and she's been the best dog we could ever hope for. Vicious? Not even close. But she is protective. She'll bark and bounce at the window when a strange adult enters the yard, just like she did in that garage all those years ago. Logically speaking, letting that man put her in my van, after witnessing her initial behavior, was a dumb move. But it turned out to be one of the best things that ever happened to our family. If I had judged Natasha's book by its cover, we would have missed out on one of the best canine companions a family could ever ask for.

~Brenda Kezar

Sweeter Than Ice Cream

The pleasant small town of Urbana, Ohio, was, and still is, so tiny that almost everyone in town knows everyone else in town. As a matter of fact, long-time residents usually know not only you but also your parents and grandparents and perhaps even your great-grandparents. One of Urbana's unheralded claims to fame is an old-fashioned ice cream parlor called Kerr's Sweet Shop, which has been in the same spot for decades. To the townspeople of Urbana, Kerr's well-worn atmosphere is as familiar and comfortable as a favorite pair of old jeans.

One young boy regularly visited this ice-cream parlor with his dog, a boxer named Gar. Gar was short for Gargantua, named after the famous giant, because he grew to be such a big dog. "Ninety-seven pounds of pure muscle!" the boy would proclaim proudly.

Whenever the boy visited the ice-cream parlor, which was almost daily in the summer, he always ordered two ice-cream cones—a chocolate one for himself and a vanilla one for Gar. A self-proclaimed "chocoholic," the boy felt badly that Gar always had to settle for vanilla, even though he knew chocolate is dangerous for dogs. Of course, Gar didn't seem to mind; he wagged his stubby tail gleefully when the boy held out the vanilla cone for him to lick as they sat together on the steps outside the ice-cream parlor. The boy often half-joked that if they could find a way to harness the energy of that tail to a generator, they would have enough power to light all of Urbana for weeks on end.

One time, the boy was sick with the flu and wasn't able to leave the house to go to school, much less the ice-cream parlor. After four days, or maybe a full week, when he was well again, the boy took Gar out for their routine walk around town. The dog trotted happily beside him, no leash required, stopping here and there to sniff at bushes and hydrants and trees. When the pair came into view of Kerr's Sweet Shop, Gar suddenly left the boy's side and dashed across Main Street. Pausing at the far corner, he glanced back, as if imploring his owner to follow. So the boy did, following Gar right up through the door and into the ice-cream parlor.

The boy walked up to the counter, asked for "the usual," and sifted through change in his pocket to pay. But instead of "the usual" ten cents—a nickel for each cone—the man working as the ice-cream scooper said the boy owed a quarter. The boy was confused. He ordered only two single-scoop cones: one vanilla, one chocolate, just as he always did; that should be a dime.

The man smiled and said, "Well, your dog's been comin' in the past few afternoons around this time, and he kept barkin' and barkin' and wouldn't stop. We figured that, since you always get a vanilla cone for him and he likes 'em so well, we'd just give him some ice cream and keep a tab for him. I hope that's okay."

The boy laughed and assured the man that it certainly was. In fact, he told them to keep the tab running if Gar came in again by himself, which the dog occasionally did. Years later, long after he'd grown to be a man, the boy still got a kick out of telling the story about his crazy dog with his very own charge account at the local ice-cream parlor.

My grandpa was that young boy, and his story about Gar and the ice-cream parlor is one of my favorites. Ever since I was a little girl, I have begged him to tell that story over and over, wishing I had a boxer dog just like his beloved Gar. A dog I could raise from a puppy and take for walks around town and get ice cream with. A dog who would sleep at the foot of my bed at night and be my best friend.

My dad grew up listening to the same stories, and he understood how much I wanted a dog like Grandpa's Gar. Though Dad was open to the idea of getting a boxer, we lived in a small condominium that was too cramped for a big dog who loves to run and play. So, for what seemed like a very long time, my boxer dreams were just that—a little girl's heart wishes.

Then, during the summer before I went into third grade, we moved to a bigger house—with a backyard!—and suddenly my dream of owning a boxer seemed wonderfully within reach. That year, as with previous years, a boxer puppy was at the top of my birthday wish list. While we lived in the condo, I never really expected to get one. But when my first birthday in our new house arrived, I had high hopes.

Gramps came over for dinner to help us celebrate my tenth birthday. He gave me the last present himself, a book titled *Caring for Your Boxer Puppy*. I opened the cover to find a note written inside: "The real thing will be coming in a few weeks." And sure enough, on a sunny spring day a short time later, I played fetch with my new puppy, Gar, for the first time!

Gar soon proved to live up to his namesake's reputation as quite a goofy character. He often "works on his tan" while napping on the porch in the afternoon sunshine. He doesn't care much for ice cream, but he does love oatmeal cookies—not chocolate chip, though, because Gramps was quick to tell me that chocolate is bad for dogs. Gramps refers to Gar as my "brother," and he spoils him like he is indeed another grandchild. Not surprisingly, Gar absolutely adores his "grandfather."

Another thing Gar, like his predecessor, adores is going for walks around the neighborhood. If I so much as whisper the word *walk*, he immediately starts jumping around frantically and scratching at the front door in excited anticipation. If I am later than usual in asking, he lets me know he's ready to go by whining at the cupboard drawer where his leash is kept.

Every evening I take Gar for a two-mile walk around our neighborhood. We walk on a path that runs alongside an orange grove, with a view of rows upon rows of green trees stretching toward the distant hills and shimmering Pacific Ocean. My favorite time of the day to take a walk is just before dusk, when the sun is beginning to set and the California sky is filled with warm, soothing pinks and reds and golds. Though I tell Gar I am doing him a favor by walking him, the truth is it has become one of my favorite parts of the day too. It is my quiet time, when I can escape the hectic routines of the day and reflect upon my life and my dreams.

Most teenagers have a special place where they chill out and regroup—their bedroom or a specific hideout. My sanctuary moves—it is anywhere beside my dog. Walks with Gar keep me grounded and enable me to recognize and savor the little miracles of life—a tiny yellow flower blooming through a crack in the sidewalk, the innocent gleeful laughter of children playing in the neighborhood cul-de-sac, the slobbery wet kiss of a dog as he looks at you with unconditional love and devotion. Especially when I am worried or stressed or sad, walking alongside—or rather, being pulled along behind—my wacky, exuberant, "Eighty-six pounds of pure muscle" dog, who still thinks he's a puppy, always makes me feel better. Our walks allow me to reflect upon my many blessings, to be thankful for all I have—including the best birthday present ever, a gargantuan boxer who is sweeter than ice cream.

~Dallas Woodburn

The Tail of a Chesapeake

Maternal instincts run deep, and the day our new puppy arrived, he became my third child. Relic is a pure-bred Chesapeake Bay retriever. He is a lovely reddish brown with quizzical eyebrows and a sense of adventure and fun to match my own. He even sings. If he hears me singing anything, he happily joins in. He curls his lips forward in a perfect imitation of Charles Shultz's Snoopy and *wooo-woooo-wooos* right along with me.

He loves me.

One heartbreaking fall day, I drove over my beloved pup, right in the middle of my own driveway. It was raining, and I was in a hurry to pick up my children from school. As I backed up, Relic did not get out of the way in time, and I caught him with the rear tire of a three-quarter-ton truck.

My eight-month-old puppy yelped once.

My first line of defense is always my husband. He picked up on the first ring. "Hello?"

"Hi, honey. I drove over the dog, and I need you to come and help me. The kids need to be picked up from school, and the dog needs to go to the vet right away. I don't want the kids to see this."

"I'll be right there."

David arrived, stern-faced, about two minutes later. He picked up the dog, loaded him into the front seat of his truck, and drove away. I hopped into my truck and dashed off to the school.

As seriously bad luck would have it, the kids and I were headed for a kiddy play date. I held it together perfectly until the woman, whose cell phone I had just asked to borrow to call my husband, asked me why. That is when the enormity of what I had done struck home. I had driven over my sweet puppy and then sent him off in the care of my husband. This is a man who grew up on a farm and doesn't believe pets should have any amount of money spent on them. He is also familiar with the thirty-nine-cent solution to sick animals—a bullet to the head.

What have I done? I worried. I felt physically sick. After all, it was my fault the dog was hurt in the first place. I cried as I dialed the number.

"Heeello," my husband drawled.

"Where are you?"

"Back at work."

"Where's the dog?"

"At the vet's."

"Really? You took him to the vet?"

"Well, yes. I stopped at Dwight's first. After talking to Dwight for a bit, we decided I had two choices. One, shoot the dog and be done with it. Then later, deal with two upset children and one very upset wife—who, by chance, does not take these sorts of things lightly, forgets nothing, forgives even less, and will put me through misery for months, if not the rest of my life. Or, two, take the dog to the vet like she asked, accept that we're going to spend more than thirty-nine cents, and continue to live with happy children and a wife who still likes me. Dwight and I decided option two looked like my best choice. So I took the dog to the vet. The rest is up to you."

Guilt is the most expensive emotion. When you love someone, you are willing to spend two months salary on a wedding ring. In this case, I would have sold my very soul to find enough money to fix my dog. In fact, when I signed my Visa slip at the vet's office, I covered up the amount; I didn't want to know. In fact, when the bill came in the mail the next month, I never even opened it. I just called the bank and asked them to transfer enough money from the checking account to cover the balance on the credit card account.

Relic's best option was to amputate the leg just below the hip, the vet advised. He said I would feel worse about it than the dog would. He was right. I was devastated.

He said Relic would simply go to sleep with four legs and wake up with three. It would take a while for him to adjust, but otherwise, he would be like any other dog. Run, play, and be happy.

Again, he was right. Relic is the happiest dog I have ever owned. A playful and loving soul, he greets everyone who comes to our farm market with a wagging tail. On occasion he has wagged his tail so hard it has made him lose his balance in the hind end, and he topples over.

When you are pregnant, you see pregnant women everywhere. They just seem to appear out of nowhere like shiny beacons. Until Relic lost his leg, I never realized how many disabled people there were in our community. People with disabilities seem to relate to my dog at a deeper level. I have had strangers approach me to show me their missing fingers, thumbs, glass eyes, burns, or scars or sometimes to just tell me about their depression. Because of my dog, they feel brave enough to drop the pretense of being "perfect" and to show me their "flaw"—often with reverence, as if revealing a holy relic for the first time.

One man, for example, walked into the market and told me he was interested in buying a few apples but more interested in buying my dog. "Name your price," he said.

He was not the first to make such an offer. I laughed and tried to joke with him by saying, "Why?"

"This," he responded, tapping his prosthetic leg.

After finally giving in to my insistence that I would not sell my dog, the man chose to sit with Relic for a while. They went into the u-pick together and shared a hot dog and ice cream, though I doubt the man got much of it. When he finally left to go home, he hugged Relic and told him he loved him.

Missing fingers, legs, arms, eyes; severe arthritis; depression; you name it—people with any type of physical challenge seem to connect with my dog. They often marvel at how seemingly oblivious Relic is to his disability. For many, he is canine therapy.

"He seems so happy," they say.

"Of course he is," I reply as I watch my laughing canine play in the yard. "Because no one has ever told him he shouldn't be."

My happy-go-lucky, three-legged dog is an inspiration to anyone who has something to overcome. Relic is a testament of hope and survival. He is my hero.

~Allison Maher

The Gift That Keeps Giving

On my twenty-fifth birthday, my mother and sister waltzed into my hospital room with balloons, flowers, and a gift-wrapped package. When I unwrapped the box, I found it filled with Milk-Bones. I pushed them aside, carefully excavating their depth, looking for buried treasure. And there it was—a picture of a Yorkshire terrier clipped from a magazine. I looked at the creature's long, steel-colored hair—parted from the nose, down the back, to the tip of the tail—and then at my mother and sister, who were seated alongside the aluminum rails of my bed. I'd just had fusion surgery to stabilize degenerative bones in my left foot and ankle. My swollen left leg was set in a cast and elevated beneath a mountain of ice.

"Once you're back on your feet, we'll find a breeder, and you'll take your pick," my sister stated matter-of-factly. "It's time, don't you think?"

Only a few months before, my boyfriend had dumped me, and my first Yorkie had died of old age. Everyone was in agreement that losing the boyfriend was a blessing, but I was lost without my furry friend.

The memory made my heart ache and my eyes brim. "I'm touched—really, I am—but this is a very extravagant gift."

My mother patted my hand. "You're worth it," she said.

"But I don't see how I'll be able to take care of another dog when I can barely take care of myself these days." I gestured toward my bad leg, my intravenous line swinging like a jump rope over it.

"Don't worry. We'll help you. Besides, you're a dog person," my sister said. "You have too much love to give not to have one."

I sat there, gazing at the picture of the Yorkie— the tilted little head and V-shaped ears, those big, moist eyes. My mom and sister's offer was hard to resist. It seemed just the impetus I needed to hurry up and get well.

After three months of not being able to put any weight on my left leg, I learned that the fusion surgery had failed. Still in a cast and on crutches, I was told I'd need another surgery as soon as my leg had healed sufficiently. My spirits sunk lower than the temperatures that winter. But when the breeders my mother and sister had contacted a few months before called to tell me about their new litter, I felt a glimmer of hope.

"It's providential," my mother said. "If the next surgery's going to confine you for three more months, you might as well convalesce with a new best friend."

It didn't take much to convince me.

A week before my second surgery, we all paid a visit to the breeders. My sister drove my mother and me down a rolling suburban street as if it were a blacktop version of the yellow brick road. As we pulled into the driveway, we heard muffled barks and yelps coming from a split-level house, where dark silhouettes capped by triangular-shaped ears moved in virtually every window. Inside was a Yorkshire terrier wonderland, shepherded by Mark and Milo—two older men who seemed as devoted to each other as they were to their "kids," as they referred to their canine brood.

It was a challenge to navigate on crutches through an ankle-high sea of long-haired creatures—some festooned with paper wrappers, others with ribbons tied into top-knot bows—who fiercely protected their turf. The scent of disinfectant overpowered the smell of urine, as we were ushered into a dark-paneled room filled with even more Yorkies. They were in crates stacked up one on top of the other, and they yapped away like unhappy tenants in an over-crowded condominium complex.

"Give us a moment. We'll get the babies." Mark and Milo waltzed past gold cup trophies and pictures of Yorkie champions perched beside blue ribbons from the Westminster Dog Show.

While they were gone, my mother and sister helped me get settled upon the newspaper covering every square inch of the floor. Then three, ten-week-old Yorkie puppies were brought in and set loose around me. The smooth, black pups resembled one-pound rottweilers. There was a string of colored yarn tied around the neck of each puppy: Priscilla was sporting cotton-candy pink; Isabella, sunflower-petal yellow; Jonathan, Chianti red. The girls showered me with affection. They jumped and wriggled around too much for me to grab them. Jonathan hung back—alert and curious, yet much more reticent than his sisters.

"I like their names," I said, eyeing each puppy.

"The bitch's owner named them after her three children," Mark announced. "The real Priscilla and Isabella are beauties, but Jonathan just got his nose pierced—that, after cutting his hair into a mohawk."

"Adolescence!" Milo sighed, with a roll of his eyes.

Puppy Jonathan appeared the antithesis of his namesake. Set apart from his siblings, he sat still and erect like an aristocratic British gentleman awaiting formal introduction.

When the girls became smitten with the shoelace on my right sneaker, Jonathan finally made his break. With his short, docked tail standing tall, he scampered over and nestled inside the crux of my crossed legs like a king safely perched inside a castle. I muffed my fingers through his shiny coat, and when his sweet, gentle eyes gazed up at me, I scooped him up and brought him closer. A tiny streak of light hair shone around each side of his face like copper-colored lightening bolts emerging from a dark night sky.

Smiling at my mother and sister, I said, "He's the one."

Jonathan was completely different from my first Yorkie. He didn't bark. He didn't jump. Most times, his feet never even touched the ground. He was basically a lap dog, whom I had to coax onto the small deck off my living room three times a day. Once he'd taken care of business, he'd hurry back inside. While he was an attentive, devoted companion, he was never a bundle of energy. Maybe it was because I was immobile and confined, but sometimes I'd throw one of his toys or a ball and the only muscles that moved were those in his neck and in his eyes, as he'd simply watch the trajectory of the object in flight. It only made me love him all the more.

Shortly after I learned that my second surgery, on my foot, had failed, I was diagnosed with breast cancer. I had a partial mastectomy, followed by another foot surgery. Jonathan remained a calm, captive companion. For hours, he cuddled beside me. Yet, as my fingers eased through his silky hair, I longed for a better life than the one I had been living. Everything seemed to be on hold, and I wanted to accomplish more on a daily basis than just walking across the hall to the bathroom.

"The minute I get this thing off, we're blowing this joint—you hear me, Jono?" I knocked on my knee-high cast. The inky pools of his eyes gazed my way while he gnawed on a chew stick. "Once I'm back on my feet, we're taking walks—to the park, the mall, the library, downtown. You're coming everywhere with me."

A few months later, I crutched into the kitchen and when I looked down, I was surprised to find Jonathan's nose plunged into his water bowl. The way his paws were splashing the water from inside the bowl, it was as though he were trying to do the Australian crawl in his version of a kiddie pool. Once

I was able to pull him away, I realized he wasn't play-ing. His body started to quake and then he froze up, his legs stiffly outstretched and his eyes fixed open-wide, like he had just seen a vision of Armageddon.

Many tests later, the vet concluded the culprit— liver shunt, a condition which caused seizures.

"I certainly can't afford surgery for him. What's the alternative?"

"A modified diet and medication. But I'm not going to lie to you," the vet said. "You have a very sick little dog."

I felt an ache in my heart. "How long do you think he has?"

"It's hard to tell. If you keep close tabs, you might get a few years—five, if you're lucky." The vet turned down the corners of his mouth into a frown. "Why don't you just take him home and love him for as long as you can."

In the cab, I held Jonathan close. As all five pounds of him lay snuggled in my arms, I stroked the copper-colored hair on the crown of his head. His body felt tired and limp, and I could tell he was as worn out as I looked in the rearview mirror of the taxi—the dark circles under my eyes, the peach fuzz peaking out from beneath the bandanna on my head. I never realized how much Jonathan and I had in common. We had names with eight letters—three vowels, five consonants. At one point, we had long, silky, brown hair. Now we had been drafted into a battle of physical challenges that served to heighten a sense of our own mortality.

I thought back to the day at the breeders' when Jonathan had won my heart. I wondered if his reticence and passivity had less to do with his personality and more to do with the fact that he was born with a genetic condition. But even if that were the case, I could never regret my decision in picking him from the litter. His presence in my life had been such a gift. We loved each other without expectation and beyond our limitations. Perhaps we were brought together as kindred spirits who needed and understood each other perfectly. That's why I vowed to do right by him until the end.

Keeping Jonathan healthy and functional became a hobby of sorts. I read and researched, monitored his diet and medications, and held him close and iced him down during each harrowing seizure. He continued to thrive. When he lived past the five-year mark, the vet would greet him as "the miracle dog," scratching his head, stymied.

Though I was now cancer-free, the third surgery on my left foot failed. Finally, the fourth foot surgery produced a successful fusion. By then, however, I had similar problems with the right foot, which also required surgical repair. But I soldiered on, determined to get back on my feet and deliver on the promise I had made to Jonathan—even if it took me another four tries, which it did.

On Jonathan's tenth birthday, I bought him a red harness leash, and my mother, sister, Jonathan, and I finally set out for the park. Though his dark hair was now interspersed with silver strands, he was as energetic as a mouse on a string, zigzagging this way and that. His tail wagged continuously, and he eagerly explored everything in his path. Even though I still walked with splints and crutches, it felt exhilarating to breathe the fresh air and to be out and about. Along the way, we even made new friends, who fawned over Jono. He ate up the attention—and so did I.

"How old is your puppy?" one stranger asked. When I told her my "puppy" was ten years old, she chuckled in astonishment and leaned down to ruffle Jono's bangs. His pink tongue lapped at her hand, and he looked as though he were smiling.

That marked the first of many walks for Jonathan and me. Every time we set out, we went a little farther. Together, we navigated the twists and turns and hills and valleys on the path of life. To this day, I still wonder whether I was walking him or he was walking me.

~Kathleen Gerard

If He Only Had a Brain

When people ask me if my dog is a mutt, I tell them, "No, he's a moron."

King Louie is a ten-year-old, twelve-pound toy poodle who has the intelligence of rock salt. He was six months old when we brought him home, and he was already set in his ways. His original name was Zippy, but within days we realized the name did not suit him. We also realized we needed the help of a professional, so we enrolled him in obedience training. At the very first class, the instructor declared Louie to be untrainable. That was just after she ripped out most of her hair and right before she called him Jell-O brain and ran from the building sobbing. Louie not only flunked the class, he was dishonorably discharged.

Soon after the obedience-training debacle, we dubbed the cantankerous canine King Louie, not because of his regal demeanor or his majestic appearance, but because of his overbearing ways. The domineering little devil rules our home with an iron paw. He demands absolute respect from his human subjects. When someone attempts to usurp his authority, Louie changes from cute little fur ball to ferocious beast in 3.5 milliseconds flat. He snarls viciously at those who dare to extricate him from his couch throne.

In addition to being a control freak with a brain the size of a Rice Krispie, King Louie is also a loner. He hates drop-in guests—or any guests, for that matter. Perhaps his disagreeable temper is the result of painful periodontal disease. Or maybe he's not getting enough fiber in his diet. Whatever the reason, the toothless little tyrant discourages intruders by baring his shriveled gums and growling obscenities.

Though his domain covers forty wooded acres, the king doesn't roam very far from home. In fact, he doesn't care to go outside much at all, especially unescorted. And he is adamant about not venturing forth in the rain. It takes three sumo wrestlers to force this dwarf of a dog out the door during inclement weather. Being a passive-aggressive pooch, Louie retaliates by relieving himself on the front porch.

Louie has made his mark—several, in fact—not on the world, but in our home. Though he can roam free in our 3,000-square-feet, two-story house, when he feels the urge to throw up or have an uncontrollable bout of explosive diarrhea, he heads straight for the Oriental rug. If we toss him outside, he stands staring at the door until we let him back in. Once inside, he picks up where he left off and resumes spurting something out one end or the other. Louie faithfully obeys the doggie code of ethics, which lists Rule Number One as "*never* regurgitate outside."

The mangy monarch monopolizes my bed and whines at the bathroom door when I'm in the tub. He jumps on my lap when I'm typing, and he watches me when I go to the bathroom. He clings to me like a hair on a grilled-cheese sandwich.

Louie's favorite bone is my ankle. After nine years of intensive training, he hasn't yet learned to sit. In fact, he barely knows how to stand. However, he does respond to a few voice commands. For instance, when I say "come," he instantly runs in the opposite direction. When I say "stay," he leaps up and attaches himself, leech-like, to my thigh. When I order him to "heel," he gnaws on my shoes. When he chases cars, and I yell, "No!" he immediately steps up his pace. I can't get him to fetch either. The only stick he's interested in is a bread stick, and the only balls he'll chase are meatballs.

I think the problem is that Louie doesn't

understand English. Since poodles come from France, I tried speaking French to him. Who knew he wasn't bilingual? When I said, "Oui, oui," he did just that—on my new La-Z-Boy recliner!

This high-strung hound turns up his royal nose at Milk-Bone biscuits and dog chow, preferring instead French fries, cherries jubilee, and linguine in clam sauce. This is one thing we have in common. In fact, we're a lot alike in the eating department. Neither of us relishes what is nutritious, and we both occasionally eat till we're sick. I, however, do not gobble food whole or throw up twice my body weight—in bed, no less. Neither do I stubbornly plant myself under the dining room table, while whining, yipping, and drooling throughout the meal. I also refuse to ingest paper plates, no matter how sumptuous they smell, and I would never curl up on dirty underwear or nibble on my husband's feet.

Recently, His Peskiness accompanied us on a long car trip. A very long trip. At least it seemed to last forever. This was supposed to be a relaxing vacation? Louie refused to sit anywhere in the car but on my lap. During the six-hour trip, he busied himself by jumping in my face, licking my face, and breathing in my face. He also whined nonstop, except during an occasional break or two to lick the windows.

Riding in the car is one of Louie's favorite pastimes. Or at least he bounds enthusiastically into the car in anticipation of the ride. He believes very strongly that he must accompany us everywhere. After all, you never know when you might need a tiny demon dog to pant and bark violently right in your ear at nothing while he's walking on your chest as you speed down the expressway. The only thing Louie likes better than getting into the car is getting out. Once we leave the driveway, the pitiful whining begins and doesn't stop till the car door opens, allowing his escape. You can always tell when Louie's been in the car. The windows are coated with dog slobber, and the vehicle smells like a combination of moldy swamp water, an old bowling shoe, and a backed-up toilet.

Besides road trips, other things Louie enjoys are marking his territory when new furniture is added to our home, sitting in the middle of a room full of company and licking himself, barking incessantly at invisible monsters, violently charging the poor UPS man, routinely emitting foul odors, and ignoring everything spoken by his master, with the exception of the words *treat* and *yummies*.

A pomegranate is smarter than Crazy Louie (a.k.a. Nutsie), and any self-respecting fruit would be insulted to be compared to him. The runt is fortunate he's cute. If not for his floppy ears and that helpless, innocent look, he would never have survived this long.

The only reason we have endured "the doofus" for nine years is that we're certain no normal family would tolerate his obnoxious behavior. We empathize with him, because he is brain-damaged and ill-mannered. We wonder whether his "inner puppy" may have been traumatized early in life, warping his personality and making his applesauce-brain psychopathic. We spoil him rotten, because we feel sorry for him. He's treated better than most children, and nothing is expected of him. He doesn't even take out the garbage.

I've tried several times to give Louie away, but at the last minute, guilt always makes me back out. I just know he would drive any other owners mad. When we're tempted to get rid of him, we always reconsider after thinking about what a new owner might do when the little creep not only bites the hand that feeds him but also takes a leak on clean laundry, eats underwear, or barfs on a pillow.

So we've kept Louie all these years, not so much because we love him as to protect him from an early entrance to doggie heaven. Although, if such a place does exist, I seriously doubt that Louie would be allowed in.

~Marsha Mott Jordan

Bellatrix

On our first date, Chuck described his dog, Bellatrix, named after Orion's left shoulder and one of the brightest stars in the sky. In Latin, *bellatrix* means "female warrior."

Intrigued that Chuck was, like me, interested in Latin, astronomy, and dogs—in the same ascending order—I asked, half-joking, "Is she ferocious?"

"No," Chuck laughed. "Bell's a devoted, one-man dog—she pays no attention to anyone else."

Chuck and I continued to date, often enjoying nature walks with Bell. Never formally trained, Bell naturally heeled by Chuck's side unless invited to explore. Half elkhound, half husky, her stature inspired respect from passersby, whom she eyed noncommittally. To me she was civil, but Chuck's initial description of her as a devoted one-man dog with little interest in others seemed true.

Bell's intelligence revealed itself in her calm bearing, cool appraisal of me, and the way she turned up her nose when we first met and I foolishly spouted baby talk. I knew of relationships that had literally gone to the dogs when couples and their canines didn't bond, and for Chuck's and my relationship to last, I wanted Bell's approval.

During Chuck's first home-cooked dinner at my place, he grumbled when I set a plate on the floor for Bell. "She eats dog chow," he informed me. But she loved the roast-beef scraps, and her interest in, if not her regard for, me seemed to rise a notch.

The following spring, Chuck landed a good job managing an environmental research project and moved 100 miles to be near the agency's headquarters for training before transferring to a remote research station. I missed Chuck—and Bell. Chuck wrote how he missed me, too, especially when he and Bell walked along a nearby estuary filled with birds, how Bell was in heaven. I knew she didn't miss me at all.

In July, Chuck proposed. I joyfully agreed, suppressing doubt: Would Bell tolerate a newcomer to her pack, or would she gladly get rid of me the first chance she got?

In August, Bell got her chance. Chuck invited me to dinner in the city to make wedding plans.

"Let's meet at my apartment. I'll leave a key

under the mat in case you arrive first. Keep in mind, the place is no great shakes."

He'd already described the only month-to-month rental he'd been able to find that allowed dogs: a squat, roach-infested, cinder-block cell amid an extrusion of identical squat, roach-infested, cinder-block cells lining a freeway not far from Mickey's Blue Room, a ramshackle dive.

"Is that safe?" I asked. "Leaving a key?"

"Nobody bothers the place with Bell there."

"She might not like me invading her turf."

"She won't bite. She likes you."

Like kid-smitten parents, dog owners tend to view their canine companions as nothing but cute, cuddly, and innocent.

"I'll wait outside."

"It's sort of a seedy location."

"You just said it was safe."

"With Bell."

I timed my arrival to coincide with Chuck's estimated arrival home. Knocking at his door, I saw his entire apartment through its one and only window: few furnishings, open bathroom door, and Bell, yelping like a piston on the other side of the pane.

"Hi, Bell. Hi, Bellatrix," I crooned as I lifted the mat, found the key, turned it into the knob, and cracked the door. "Remember me? Roast-beef lady? I'm sorry I forgot to bring treats."

Bell added hip-wagging to her barking, and I regretted having to disappoint her hope for food. Patting her, I spotted a note propped on the table: "If you're reading this, I'm delayed and hurrying. Make yourself comfortable."

I gave myself the grand, ten-second tour.

Flanked by threadbare curtains more bare than thread, light from the north-facing window scarcely penetrated the tiny concrete confine. The flimsy door, held shut by a push-button lock and chain latch, was the only entry and exit. On the opposite wall, a windowless cubby with a toilet and shower provided scant privacy. In the corner that served as a kitchen, a naked metal box where a phone could be connected reminded me that Chuck hadn't ordered phone service, since he'd soon be moving to the research station. A sofa sagged below the window. Perched on it, I patted Bell's head.

Our relationship hadn't reached muzzle-nuzzling, belly-rubbing familiarity, and my patting remained circumspect. "Where's Daddy, girl? Are you lonely? When your daddy and I get married, you and I will become great friends."

She stared out the window.

Great, I sighed, *I've offended her.*

I followed her gaze and glimpsed a red and black shirt zip by.

"Watching for Chuck?" I ventured to scratch under her chin, and she closed her eyes.

Scratching and gazing out the window, I spotted the same red and black. A bearded, shaggy man ambled past, then doubled back, passing slowly—eyes locked on mine—until he disappeared from view. No doubt he saw I was alone. *What would I do if he forced his way in?* Glancing about, I thought, *Get a grip. Chuck's on his way. Even if I had a phone, what would I say?—"Help, a man passed by?"*

A bang at the door caused Bell to jump to attention and bray. Two arms-length away, the man ogled me through the pane, hoisted his jowls, and leered.

Adrenalin sparked lightning calculations: He could mean harm, so I shouldn't open the door. But then, his massive bulk could surely topple it with a single shove. At five-feet-four and 110 pounds, I surely posed no threat to this person, and he seemed not to fear Bell. My instincts commanded: DON'T COWER! I flashed a prayer for courage—or at least bravado.

Hoping she'd forgive me, I gripped Bell's collar, pretending she was vicious, and threw open the door.

"What?" I let my tone clang, irritated, hard.

As if on cue, Bell downshifted from barking to a deep, businesslike growl.

Good girl! I silently sang.

"Manager sent me to fix your wiring." Without a toolbox, he swept his eyes up and down my body.

Risking Bell's biting me, I adjusted my grip on her collar, as if I had to work to hold her back. "The tenant's not here. Come back later."

"I'm s'posed to fix it now."

Thankful as Bell fixed her growl and eyes on the man, I too looked him straight in the eye and held my voice firm. "Later."

With my free hand, I started to close the door. A look of doubt crossed the man's face, but I kept my expression unruffled, bored, while my mind whirled. *Would this stranger stick to his pretence and let me close the door? Would he hurt Bell? Would I see Chuck again? Would we get married, be a family?* I knew with sick certainty that whatever this stranger decided now would forever change my future.

His eyes brushed past Bell and me.

He stepped forward.

My ploy had failed.

By the time his foot touched ground, Bellatrix transformed into a dog I'd never seen. Clutching her collar, unsure how long I could restrain her, I stared: teeth jack-hammered, saliva flew, toes splayed, nails clawed, fur spiked, every muscle taut for attack.

The man froze.

If he moved an inch, I'd threaten to let go—forewarning him as much for *his* safety as my own. Bell strained to leap. Whatever this stranger meant to do, Bell's intentions were clear.

"Can you control that thing?" His leer slipped, his voice crunched like gravel under car tires.

"Maybe." My tone hit the mark of perfect indifference.

He edged back, turned, and rushed away. I swung the door shut, locked it, and sank to the floor. Bell licked me frantically. I hugged her tight. Comrades-at-arms, we were buddies for life.

That evening, across the restaurant table, Chuck—watching me set aside half my steak to bring home to Bell—frowned, "There's no wiring problem."

He squeezed my hand, attempting a smile. "You were saved by the Bell."

I squeezed back and raised my glass. "To Bellatrix, female warrior and my lucky star."

~*Marla Doherty*

My Black-and-White Wonder

It wasn't the combination of too much wine and not enough umbrellas. It wasn't the warm summer's evening or the satisfaction of having prepared a special family meal with no flops. My heart was full of bittersweet emotion over the sight of my mother and mother-in-law standing arm-in-arm for the first time in the more than a decade that my husband, David, and I had been married.

I have never been able to put my finger on why these two loving and nurturing mothers have remained distant. They have so much in common. If nothing else, they share two incredible grandchildren. They both love family get-togethers and traditions. They glow with joy over fruitful summer gardens and the comforts of home and hearth in the dead of winter.

Maybe now I'll never need to know. Maybe it wasn't that they didn't get along; maybe they'd never before felt the need to get together. Or maybe it isn't always the joy in life that brings people together; maybe sometimes it's sadness that is equally shared. After all, there they were now, locking arms over the loss of a shared love for an ornery, black-eared Dalmatian named Louie.

Long before I'd met David, Louie was the guy who filled my heart and turned my little apartment into a home. He was the guy I came home to and woke up with, and the companion who gladly hopped in the car and came along on all of my errands. He was my partner and family, all in one shedding bundle of black and white. I took him on road trips through the mountains and on beach vacations. In December, we'd go sit on Santa's lap, and one year he even smiled for the camera.

Louie filled me up when I needed it the most, and my parents had been relieved, I'm sure, that someone could do that for me. In kind, they gratefully took him in when we came back to the nest for a while. My stepdad, a retired marine, took him to the park every night for some basic military training. My mom gladly embraced him, even though all of her furniture (well, all of her everything) became accessorized with prickly white hairs.

The morning after our first date, David showed up to take Louie and me out for breakfast. No kidding—we went to a sidewalk café, and David ordered a slice of Canadian bacon and a bowl of water for Louie. After David and I fell in love, David admitted that my black-and-white cupid had stolen his heart even before I did. Luckily, he came to love me as well. A year or so later, Louie was brought to the church for our wedding pictures, bowtie and all.

During one snowy Christmas Eve drive to David's childhood home, I turned around to check on Louie and saw that the back seat was covered in blood. So many thoughts raced through my head: *Do we turn back or keep going? Will David's hometown vet still be open? How will my mother-in-law react to having her lovely house exposed to a bloody dog on Christmas Eve?* I shouldn't have worried. One phone call, and it was all taken care of. My mother-in-law wouldn't hear of us turning around. She arranged for the vet to stay open (I think she even paid the bill.), and she spread some old towels around her house. In a day or two, Louie was all fixed up and ready to run off his Christmas dinner.

When it finally came time for David and I to have a more traditional family—a baby boy, then a baby girl—Louie became a reluctant big brother. He'd had me all to himself for so long, he initially didn't like those noisy, pink siblings that kept me too busy to play. Yet, he would dutifully hop in the minivan and go wherever it was that we seemed to always be going. There is a black-and-white blurred blob in every picture I snapped during those years, and these days, when I sit down to look at photo albums, I couldn't be happier to see him.

Somewhere along the line, my Louie turned into crotchety old man. Rather than hopping into the car, he waited to be hoisted. He wasn't my familiar shadow on the many trips up and down the stairs; instead, he would look longingly up at me from the bottom of the stairs, willing me to come back down. When the day came that I found him eating his dinner while lying down, I knew I had to make the call.

I slept on the floor downstairs with him that last night, hoping in the morning the vet would say I was wrong, that it wasn't time for Louie to leave us. So when I kissed him and waved as my husband drove away with him, I told myself, *They might be back. . . . They might be back.*

David came back alone, very shaken. In hindsight, I shouldn't have asked him to do what I'd always considered to be my job. I just didn't think I could bear it.

As it turned out, another thing I couldn't bear was to scatter his ashes anywhere until I was sure that we were "home." The house we were living in at the time was our starter house, and surely we would be moving on at some point. I wanted to have Louie with us always.

So there we were, more than five years later, standing in the rain in the wooded backyard of our new home, some 120 miles away from the house we'd lived in when we lost Louie. We had packed up and moved twice since then, each time bringing along the wooden box that held my first companion.

My parents were visiting from Florida. My in-laws were happy to accept our invitation to dinner. And my vision of finally having a family night that included both of our children's grandmothers was in clear view. We would eat, marvel over the children, and then what? What if there was dead air and my mom and mother-in-law had nothing to say to each other? Worse yet, what if I could sense their discomfort over being in each other's company after a decade apart?

I had a plan, one that fulfilled a long-held dream. Since we knew that we had finally found the home that would nurture not only David and me and our two children, but also a menagerie of animal family members for years to come, how about a pet cemetery?

So on that rainy summer's evening, with full bellies and full hearts, two families finally became one as we stepped through the wet grass out to what would become Louie's final resting place. One by one, we each recalled our favorite memories of my first true love, each reminiscence bringing a smile or even a laugh. While looking at my two moms sharing an umbrella, arm-in-arm, it occurred to me just how strong the love of animals can be—in our case, stronger than hundreds of miles, two births, and over a decade of memories. That night, one family was finally born of two.

~*Julie Clark Robinson*

The Human Whisperer

My husband likes to tell people that I married him for his dog. I always say that's ridiculous, but Kipper looks at me with a look on her intelligent face that seems to say, "Your secret's safe with me, Alpha Mom."

Six years ago, I was unaware of the magic some canines possess. As time went by, I discovered that dogs have their own language of romance, and it has nothing to do with Frank Sinatra or Godiva chocolates. When my husband and I started dating, his yellow Labrador retriever also began courting me. I never stood a chance. Whenever Tim would invite me over for a romantic dinner, Kipper would make plans to woo me with anticipation and play. I'd hear how much my presence meant when I'd arrive.

"That dog has been lying in front of the garage door for more than an hour waiting for you," Tim would say while Kipper would wag her tail and flash me a big dog smile. I'd scratch her behind her velveteen ears, impressed with such devotion. *What man would ever wait by a phone or door?* I'd wonder. While my beau would cook a gourmet meal and pour me a glass of wine, Kipper would offer me one of her dog toys, an equivalent gesture in her world. I'd offer her a doggie appetizer from her treat jar, and she'd sit politely and take it from my fingertips. She'd teach me interactive games such as fetch, tug, and chase-a-dog. I also learned that we shared a common trait— the ability to be silly. Meeting a man with a sense of humor had been wonderful; I'd never counted on meeting a dog with one too. Lucky me.

As the relationship between Tim and me grew more serious, Kipper started expecting more commitment on her end. She would get more distressed whenever I'd visit and then leave to go home.

"That dog has grown really fond of you," Tim would say, shaking his head. "She doesn't understand why you're going."

I'd see Kipper's expressive face change from happy to disappointed. She would have been a great silent-movie star. Every time I'd leave, I swear I could hear her trying to persuade me to stay: "But wait. I was going to make espresso. Bow-wow."

I began experiencing my first pangs of dog

abandonment guilt, a well-known affliction to dog owners, but a new feeling for me. I had it bad, and that wasn't good. *How could I convince her I wasn't just a play-with-a-dog-toy-and-leave-'em kind of gal?* I'd wonder.

Fortunately, Tim proposed, and we were married the following year. During our wedding ceremony, I imagined the reverend handing me one of Kipper's toys during the exchange of wedding bands. "And do you take this yellow, rubber ring-a-ding as a token of Kipper's love?"

Before we moved into our new house, I picked up Kipper one day and drove her there to introduce her to the new environment, hoping to reduce any shock when we moved in. I was worried that she'd be upset to leave the house she'd lived in since she'd been a puppy.

"We're all going to move in here together soon, Kipperdog," I told her, taking off her leash to let her walk around. "What do you think?"

Her snout went crazy as she ran through the empty place, investigating every inch. She wagged her powerful tail, looking pleased. Later, I told Tim about our preliminary visit and how relieved I was at Kipper's positive response. He just laughed. "You spoil that dog. She'll be happy to be wherever you are," he said.

When we settled into our new nest together as husband and wife, I became an official dog mom. Kipper was thrilled to finally have me where she felt I'd always belonged, with her and Alpha Dad. We became one happy pack in her eyes, and after three years of marriage, the romance hasn't ended.

This old dog is still full of surprises and willing to learn new tricks. She's twelve-"Labradorable"-years old now, and we have special rituals and a communication style of our very own. Every morning when I get up, she greets me with a big dog hug, nuzzling her furry body against me while I wrap my arms around her and tell her what a good dog she is. Every night at bedtime, she trots over to her big dog nest for flat-dog time. Tim and I give her a kiss and a tuck-in. If she were a cat, she would purr.

Every time we come back inside after conducting dog business in the yard, she likes celebrating her achievement. She picks up a toy, puts all four paws to the floor, and takes off in wild circles around the couch, taunting me to try and catch her. This goofy behavior is also displayed after dog baths and towel rubdowns. *We should all feel that good,* I think, *envious of her ability to live in each moment and truly appreciate it.*

Holidays and special occasions are memorable times for this festive dog. She enjoys wearing a black cape for Halloween and greeting trick-or-treaters at the front door. Birthdays mean presents, which also offer her another benefit. She loves ripping wrapping paper and gift bags to shreds, bit by bit, a messy indulgence we allow her on those days. It's a dog thing, I guess.

She's also a dog of a thousand faces and loves posing for me. I keep a camera handy to catch as many of her expressions as possible. One of my favorite shots is of her wearing a jaunty St. Patrick's Day hat. Even though she's not crazy about hats, she'll wear them for me for special photo ops.

Every time Kipper gazes at me with those big, chocolate, give-me-another-treat eyes of hers, I realize that it's a miracle that she doesn't weigh 200 pounds. In the kitchen, she's my cooking muse and sous chef, consuming leftover bites of chopped veggies and offering new recipe ideas, often involving pork. She'll sprawl out on her belly on the floor and eat a whole cored apple without using her paws. Wolfgang Puck, eat your heart out.

Tim shakes his head sometimes while observing dog and Alpha Mom at work or play. As Kipper follows me around the house like a lovesick teenager, he sighs and says, "You're not Daddy's dog anymore."

"She's just protective of me," I respond.

"That's more than protection," he says. "That's love."

Whenever I see the way she looks at me, I know he's right. Some days, I'm still amazed that we share our walls with this mysterious, four-legged creature, who seems to understand everything we say. We call her the "human whisperer." Kipper, the Wonderdog, humbles me daily with her devotion and patience. She's a loving and empathetic soul who always has time to listen to us, even though we don't always have time for her. No scale exists that can measure the depth of her love.

Dogs can do that if you're not careful—sneak into your heart over time and capture it forevermore.

~Julie Matherly

Sonata for Bach

Every morning, bright and early, as golden rays of sunshine pierce through the white lace curtains of our kitchen window, I am greeted with the same string of musical notes, sung by my blonde cocker spaniel, Bach, named after my favorite composer, Johann Sebastian Bach. After his recital of high-pitched shrieks, Bach launches a barrage of lightening attacks with his nose and paws at the basement door, until I set him free.

I sometimes wonder if he has an alarm clock in his head. Each morning, at the same time, he is by the basement door, waiting for me to come into the kitchen. When I open the door, he sits in the doorway for a few moments, licks his paws, and looks around arrogantly with his big black eyes, as though it were not all that important to be released.

Usually I ignore him while I make my breakfast,

though I can feel his eyes, watching, watching, watching. Only when I sit down at the table to eat breakfast does he take flight, and his journey around the room always ends up in the same place—on my lap, after a little ritualistic dance and a nudge of his nose at my arm. The nudge is to tell me to hurry up with breakfast. After the nudge, he nestles comfortably in my lap and waits patiently until I've eaten my breakfast, so we can go about the business of the day.

Bach is my companion to the post office and grocery store and on my morning walk around the block. As soon as I say, "Let's go for our walk," he dashes to get his leash and brings it to me. When we get to the path along the golf course, I remove him from the leash, and he leads the way. He knows the route by heart, well marked by every tree or post he relieved himself on the day before. Running ahead, he explores everything around him, enjoying the warmth of the sun and the birds singing in the trees. On rainy days, he refuses to stay under the umbrella with me, preferring to be out in the rain, dancing in the puddles, barking and biting at the raindrops.

Bach sits beside me on the couch when I watch movies. He laughs with me through comedies and is terrified by horror movies, during which he cuddles up against the side of my leg for safety. When I have popcorn, he perches eagerly beside me, trying to eat his share. Sometimes I toss a kernel onto the floor, and he quickly dives down to fetch it. After a few times, he gets mad, takes the piece of popcorn, and hides it beneath the sofa.

Bach always has a smile on his face and a sweet word to say in his own language, a language I am slowly starting to understand. When I go to the kitchen, he follows; when I go to the bathroom, I can see his shadow beneath the door on the other side, pacing back and forth. At night when I put him in the basement, he gazes at me with saddened eyes, like a small child who wants to sleep with his parents. However, my wife will not allow it. She often swears to God that I love that dog more than I love her. That is not true; I love them the *same*, but I would never tell her that.

The other day on the way to the grocery store, Bach started to jump around frantically on the seat of my old sedan, barking at the top of his voice. I'd never seen him act that way before. It was if he were having a panic attack.

"What's wrong, Bach?" I asked.

He looked at me as though I was supposed to understand his ranting, and then he jumped into the back seat, performed a little dance, and ran back and forth across the seat, barking loudly.

"Chill out," I said with a little smile, not taking my eyes off the road.

Bach screamed again and again. I realized he was trying to tell me something important, but I could not understand what it was. He leaped back up to the front seat, ran to me, and pushed at my arm with his nose.

"Relax, take it easy," I said.

He raced to the side window, sat with his paws on the edge of the door, and barked out the window frantically.

"What's wrong?" I asked again, growing concerned.

Bach turned quickly, gazed at me with a look that sent a chill up my spine and made the hairs on the back of my neck stand on end. I knew there was something wrong.

"Okay, you win," I muttered, as I quickly pulled over to the side of the road. Just as I turned off the ignition, a big yellow cargo van appeared out of nowhere. It sped by the path I'd been on, hitting a parked car and flying up over the curb before coming to rest in the flowerbed of a big white house across the street.

I sat, wide-eyed and taking deep breaths. Bach sat on my lap, licking at my trembling hands gripped tightly around the steering wheel. The comforting stroke of his tongue finally made me relax, and I was able to get out of the car and run over to the truck.

I was relieved to discover that no one had been hurt in the accident. I also learned that the truck's brakes had given out and were making a high-pitched squeal as the truck raced toward me. It was this sound that Bach had picked up on and was frantically trying to warn me about. Though my wife is grateful to Bach for barking me out of harm's way and possibly saving my life, she still insists that he sleep in the basement. But I've decided he can have all the popcorn he wants when we watch movies together.

~Robert Rohloff

Clod of My Heart

I t was a beautiful Saturday morning in spring. The trees were dancing in the breeze, a cue to grab my windbreaker. I sighed as I slipped it on. If only I didn't need to get the mail. Going outside alone, for any reason, was no longer an option for me; it was a doggie event . . . a double-doggie event. When I sat down on my bed and started putting on my sneakers, both dogs scurried to their leash basket. As usual, Syco trampled over Butkus, smushing his arthritic back-end, causing it to go flat as a pancake, as if it were boneless.

"Stop stepping on your brother, you clod!" I yelled, shaking my head in disgust, for the umpteenth time.

Butkus was my favorite dog, and I didn't attempt to hide it. He was my heart. And Syco was . . . well, a royal pain in my neck.

I hadn't even wanted him, knowing Butkus was the only dog for me. I was so attached to my sweet old Labrador retriever that my husband, Chuck, would sometimes wonder whom I loved more: man or beast. Chuck was definitely not the top dog the day he uttered those awful words: "You know, Beth, Butkus is getting older. He won't live forever. We should get you another dog."

No dog could replace Butkus!

Not long after, though, we welcomed . . . well, Chuck welcomed . . . home our new bouncing baby rottweiler. Poor Syco never stood a chance; the competition was just too great. My heart belonged to Butkus, and it never really warmed to Syco. For two years he'd done his best to emulate his favored stepsibling. But to me, he was still the pain-in-the-neck "Cinderfella" who never ceased to annoy me—like when he bowled over Butkus, again, in his zeal to accompany us to the mailbox.

I clipped on the leashes and headed down the driveway. Syco is a perfect soldier on his leash. He'd better be, after the bucks we forked out for the two-week doggie boot camp he'd attended to make him that way. Syco has the same disposition as Butkus. They are both sweet, gentle, loving dogs. But that's were the similarities end. While Syco is a handsome, energetic, slobbering, 150-pound tank of purebred rottweiler, Butkus is a generic black Lab, grizzled from age, with ten pounds of benign fatty tumors all over him—gorgeous only to me.

When the two dogs and I stepped outside, the children playing in our cul-de-sac headed toward us. I knew they were coming to look at the giant dog I hadn't allowed them to play with since he was a puppy. I put Syco in a sit-stay command. In one swift move, I unhooked his leash, looped it through the handle of one of the emptied Rubbermaid garbage cans sitting at the curb, and then reattached the leash to his collar. Knowing Syco was the better-trained dog, I figured he would stay put and visit with the kids while I went with Butkus to get the mail.

As I walked to the mailbox, I noticed there were kids everywhere. At least a dozen lived on the street, and they all seemed to have friends over today. I looked back at Syco, still sitting proudly in his sit-stay command, happily awaiting the arrival of his newfound friends. *Ah, he'll be fine,* I reassured myself. *He's leashed to the can, and I'm only a few feet away. And thanks to that boot camp diploma, he listens to commands.*

Derek's voice rose above the others. Seven years old and extremely bright, he wasn't the oldest kid on the block, but the others followed him like he was the Pied Piper. "Guys, go slowly, or you'll scare him. Remember what Beth taught us. Put your palm out so he can sniff it first before you pet him. And don't pet him on the top of the head. Petting a dog on top of the head is a sign of aggression. Pet him under the neck. Got it, guys? Now, one at a time." He turned to me with a big grin. "Right, Beth? Did I forget anything?"

Complete self-confidence emanated from Derek's smiling face. I was dumbfounded. It had been ages since he'd been near Syco. I'd let the neighborhood children socialize with "the rottweiler puppy" twice, once when Syco was three months old and again when he was a year. Derek had sat in the center of the circle when I plopped the thirty-pound puppy down on my front lawn and spelled out the rules. At that first encounter, I'd told them Syco wouldn't be anything like Butkus—that he would be too big and gruff for them to play with. I'd been half-right. At a year old, Syco was huge. But he wasn't at all aggressive, and he loved people, including kids. The younger boys giggled and asked whether Syco would be an "attack" or "guard" dog when he grew up. Imagining the conversations at the dinner tables on my block that night, I gulped and answered no to both questions and then conceded Syco would be exactly like Butkus, only larger.

Now I watched from the mailbox as several other boys swarmed around Syco. Vince, Derek's older brother by two years, crept cautiously closer, as if Syco were a specimen in a zoo with a warning sign above him that read: *Please do not touch.* I kept one eye on Syco as I opened the mailbox, while Butkus circled himself around my ankles like a boa constrictor. I watched as Vince waved his hand back and forth in front of Syco's face, teasing him. Syco started to pant heavily and whimpered for a pet.

Succumbing to Syco's pathetic cry, Vince reached for the top of Syco's head to oblige, completely forgetting his brother's instructions. Syco, a timid dog, jerked back from Vince's hand, and when he did, his heavy back paw crunched down on the foot of Vince and Derek's little brother. Five-year-old Tony let out a high-pitched cry as Clod Dog proceeded to plop his entire butt down on the boy's foot. All eyes flew to a wailing, and now pinned, Tony.

Vince scrambled back in fear, his arms flailing wildly and screaming, "He bit Tony! He bit my brother!" As he continued to careen backward, trying to escape the "vicious" rottweiler, one of his arms smashed into the garbage can, which landed on Syco's head, entombing the now-terrified dog inside the can.

Syco shot off like a cannon. The momentum knocked the garbage can off his head, and it crashed to the pavement with an explosive *Bam!* Syco raced around the cul-de-sac, with the world's ugliest kite— an airborne garbage can—tethered to his collar and flopping in the wind behind him! Vince got knocked down first; he was the closest. Derek dove out of the way onto the grass. Tony and another boy were knocked to the curb, falling one after the other like dominos.

Syco picked up speed, desperate to outrun the big, scary green monster chasing after him. Tony was crying. Vince was still screaming. I was mortified. Feet cemented to the ground, I stood in horrified disbelief, watching the train wreck I had inadvertently caused.

Phyllis, the mother of the three brothers, had her mom radar on and heard her boys' cries. She ran up the sidewalk, her head swiveling as she passed Syco, who was now galloping like a wild pony in the street. Her face twisted into a comic expression when she saw her crying, screaming kids.

Syco took a sharp right and headed straight up my next-door neighbor's driveway. The garbage can remained suspended in the air behind him as he zipped between the two cars parked in the drive. He hit a dead-end when he reached the closed garage. Instantaneously, he jumped up on his hand legs, pushed off the door with his front paws, and turned to run in the opposite direction, all in one smooth motion, like a synchronized swimmer. Because the U-turn slowed his speed, there wasn't enough air to keep the garbage-can-kite afloat, and now it bounced side to side, banging into the cars, first one, then the other. The loud booms could be heard down the entire block.

The noise brought other people running out of their houses. Everyone lined up on the sidewalk, staring with mouths agape and eyes wide, watching Syco race down the street, the big green monster hot on his tail. Butkus and I still hadn't moved. I made a feeble and futile attempt to call Syco; even Butkus gave me the "You've got to be joking" face.

"Beth, quick! Go get some dog cookies," Derek said, shaking me out of my stunned stupor. "Hurry, Beth!"

Butkus and I ran into my house. I grabbed a handful of cookies, but tripped over my own feet and dropped them. I grabbed another handful and raced out the door, leaving Butkus behind to happily clean up the mess. Meanwhile, Syco went up another neighbor's driveway, did another about-face at the garage door, and repeated the boom-boom car trick. That inspired him to run even faster. When I handed the cookies to Derek, who gave me an "about time" eye-roll, he was already poised on his

Razor scooter for immediate take off, like a runner being handed off a baton in a relay race.

I watched in horror as Syco ran straight toward the children on Rollerblades. That galvanized some panicked spectators to holler at their children to get out of the way. But the kids were too busy laughing. Their laughter quickly subsided when they realized Syco was heading their way.

Please, please, please, no, Syco, no, I pleaded wordlessly. When he veered and missed the kids, I breathed a sigh of gratitude. My relief was short-lived. As Syco rounded the cul-de-sac, the flying garbage can knocked down all of the kids like bowling pins. A perfect strike! Some rolled to the grass; others landed on their butts or knees.

Suddenly, Derek appeared alongside Syco on his scooter, like a little dog-whispering cowboy, and started tossing cookies. At first, Syco kept his head forward, afraid to look beside or behind him, but then Derek got ahead of him. He kept talking to Syco and tossing him cookies. Finally, Syco began to slow down and sniff. Derek jumped off his scooter and held a cookie in front of him. Exhausted, Syco came to a dead stop and plopped down into a full belly sprawl. His tongue hung out so far, it almost licked the pavement. The cookie just sat on his dry tongue. The dented green monster lay still behind him.

Derek unhooked Syco's leash and threw his arms around the big dog's head. They sat in the middle of the street, Derek hugging Syco and speaking to him in a soothing voice. I headed toward Syco and Derek—I had damage control to do—but before I reached them, Phyllis grabbed my arm and demanded I sit with her on the curb. I was shaking from head to toe.

"Relax, Beth," she said in her comforting mom voice. "We have just a few Band-Aid situations here. Not a single car is dented. Everyone is laughing their butts off. The kids will be telling this story forever. Your garbage can is a goner, but everything else is fine. It's okay."

"It's more than what just happened. Granted, today was the big Kahoona, but it's always *something* with Syco," I said. "He's so hard to love. . . . I just don't love him like I do Butkus! I can't!"

"Well then, don't. Love them differently," she said.

I took Phyllis's advice. Butkus may be my heart, but Syco is my comic relief.

~Beth Rothstein Ambler

Strange Bedfellows

I am sixty-two years old and allergic to dogs. I never owned a dog before, much less a puppy. Yet these nights I share my lumpy mattress with a cockapoo named Buffy.

It didn't start out that way. She slept in her crate in the kitchen until an old diesel Mercedes caught fire in a driveway six feet from my leaky windows. Fumes permeated our small house. When I returned from treatment for smoke inhalation, I brought Buffy into my room to sleep; the air was slightly better there. Since then, she howls if she is not in bed with me. To tell the truth, I miss her too.

In a misguided effort to separate dog and woman, I created a special place for her at the foot of my bed, piling items for her comfort as follows: folded top sheet, waterproof pad, late son's old art project towel, and slightly chewed fleece bedding she had slept under in her crate. A smelly piece of braided yarn, a favorite toy, decorates her bed on a bed. Buffy has taken over half the remaining half bed, choosing to sleep parallel to, not atop, her special setup. I wrap myself around the remaining real estate like a disproportioned capital L. The top half of my body is positioned at a sharp angle from the bottom half, and important parts of me rest on a wayward spring in the mattress. *If the spring pokes me,* I wonder, *will I need a tetanus shot?*

People who live with dogs say their appeal is the unconditional love dogs give. But to me, the opposite is true. My dog's special appeal is her willingness to accept love from me.

I have always enjoyed simple physical intimacies: a firm handshake, a casual touch on the shoulder, a quick hug from a friend. These intimacies were taken from me when a BMW crashed into my life. No one touched me except doctors. As I became isolated at home, old friends faded away, and I had no chance to make new ones. There were no full body hugs, strokes, or casual embraces given or gotten. No one welcomed my caresses.

Now I have a pup who sits on my lap on occasion. I can touch her, pet her, and groom her. She rests at my feet so that I cannot move without her knowledge. She makes me burst out laughing. It feels so good.

Buffy is a social butterfly. My injuries had made me a hermit. Now, I return waves and smiles from passersby when we sit on the front porch. They're smiling and waving at her, but she takes me with her into the social world I had missed for so long.

To the amusement of folks around here, Buffy has two strollers. They are for my benefit, not hers, I explain in vain. Balance problems have kept me close to home; stroller handles are the right height to hang onto for support. So I pile the Buffer into a stroller and take off for widening circles around the block.

Sometimes it's a little too chilly for a dog just to sit in a stroller, so I put a red, quilted, fleece-lined jacket on her or maybe a pink turtleneck sweater with cable stitching and sequins.

"Fine dress," laughs the neighbor down the block, new to English, but able to turn a phrase or two.

"Oh, so she can walk," he said when he saw Buffy on a leash. His wife explains that the dog is a like a family member to me, and I dispute her. But how can I make my case while wearing an outfit that matches the dog's?

I had some misgivings about getting a puppy, but my doctor encouraged me to try. "Everything is harder for you," the doctor had said, "and this will be too. But just think of the possible benefit." He knew that social isolation was one of the most difficult aspects of my injury and that caring for a puppy could be just the thing to ease me back into humanity. And so I bit.

I wanted to name the pup Beautyrest, because I used my mattress money for her. The breeder dissuaded me, saying, "Imagine calling your dog. Your neighbors will think you are calling your mattress." She also vetoed Gussie as old-fashioned, even though both our grandmothers shared the name and made great stuffed cabbage. So my first-generation mix of cocker spaniel and poodle became Buffy—Buffarina Ballerina, in full.

Over the past decade of my younger son's death, two car crashes, cancer, and diabetes, I have felt my heart break. I hadn't known people could feel hearts breaking over time, pieces detaching from the whole and floating down to who-knows-where. Amazingly, Buffy is making my heart whole again.

Sometimes I just stare at her while she sleeps, trying to be quiet so as not to wake her. I search for the mechanism she uses to reattach the pieces of my heart. I like to think she works with fuzzy multicolored yarn, threaded through a wide-eyed needle, so much like the yarn and needle my mother used to finish afghans she made for anyone with a chill. Despite my search, I cannot find the instrument. But my heart heals.

Recently I stirred at night and became indignant when I felt Buffy too near to me. As close as we were together, she was clearly far out of bounds. I opened my eyes to move her, to whisper "place," and to correct her for her faux pas. Much to my surprise, I found that Buffy was where she belonged. I was the one who had migrated to intimacy.

~Marilyn A. Gelman

Who's the Boss?

For the first twenty years of my life, the most exciting pet I was permitted to own was a goldfish. Actually, two goldfish. They lived remarkably short lives and came to ignoble burials in the sewer system of New York City. I was not raised to be, by any stretch of the imagination, a dog lover.

Then I met my future husband. When Russ was in middle school he kept 100 white mice in his family's small apartment. During high school he worked in a pet store. By the time I met him he was a proud "papa" to a five-year-old, ugly, drooling, snoring, English bulldog.

I fell in love—with Russ, not the dog. Unfortunately, it was a package deal, and we became an instant family: Russ, Lord Cardigan, and I. What I didn't realize was that Lord Cardigan was only the beginning.

As the years flew by, a succession of four-legged "children" passed through our home and our lives. Alphabetically, we had Ebby, Fanny, General Montgomery, Linda, Lord Cardigan, Lacy, Pumpkin, and Romer. They represented a variety of breeds, including mutts (better known as "all-Americans"), boxers, a bull-mastiff, and a Lhasa apso.

Ebby was, by far, the smartest of them all. A shepherd-mix, he was part of a litter rescued from the streets of Brooklyn, New York, and he was one fast learner. First and foremost, he learned that Russ was a guaranteed soft touch. The hand that fed him was the same hand that played, healed, and loved.

Me? I clearly held a distant second place in Ebby's heart—and for very good reason. I was the family disciplinarian. Certain ground rules for our various adoptees had been established early in our marriage: no feeding from the table, no jumping on the furniture, no sleeping on the bed. Russ always agreed—a bit too readily, I might add—and I often wondered what happened to the rules when I wasn't home. The frequent discovery of dog hairs on our bed and in our blankets served only to fuel my suspicions.

The proof came soon enough.

One morning, Russ woke up at his usual, early-bird time of 5:00 A.M. It was still dark, and I barely stirred as he prepared for work. It was one of those rare occasions when I had the opportunity to sleep in, and I was eager to float back to the deep slumber that had been interrupted by his departure.

Moments after he left, I lay perfectly still, waiting for a comfortable haze to envelop me once again. Instead, I heard the sound of someone in the hall, the almost imperceptible whisper of padded footsteps slowly moving toward the bedroom. I froze, instantly wide awake. Had Russ forgotten something on his way to work? I hadn't heard the front door open. Did someone break into the house? Surely Ebby would have heard and barked a warning. The quiet footsteps gradually approached the open bedroom door. I lay still, tense and silent. My head just happened to be facing the door, and I fixed my gaze on the doorway.

The answer appeared a moment later. Ebby gingerly padded into view and turned to step into the bedroom. Catching a glimpse of me lying on the bed, he froze with one paw lifted in mid-air over the threshold, and then, without missing a beat, made the most graceful (and silent) U-turn I have ever witnessed. The muted whisper of his footsteps receded down the hall as he returned to his bed in the kitchen.

I laughed to myself. It was obvious that I had upset a long-standing practice, but Ebby wasn't going to let on. In fact, when I got up a few minutes later to let him out to the yard, I truly believe he was pretending to still be asleep. He opened one groggy eye (what an actor!) and greeted me with a drowsy "kiss." Although I was on to him, and he knew it, we both behaved as if nothing had changed.

If I had any remaining doubts about how well the rules were being followed, they were dispelled a few weeks later. Coming home late one night and finding the house dark, I quietly opened the front door so as not to wake Russ and tiptoed to the bedroom. I could see his silhouette as he lay sleeping. But wait . . . who—or what—was that on the bed next to him? Stepping back into the hallway, I turned on the light and once again peered into the dim room. There was no doubt about it: Ebby was curled up against Russ's legs. As I entered the bedroom, both Russ and Ebby awoke just enough to simultaneously raise their heads. Russ looked from me to Ebby and back to me again, and then shook his head as if to say, "I hope this isn't what I think it is," while Ebby merely cast a dismissive glance in my direction before laying his head back down. Then, without a sound, both of them closed their eyes and returned to sleep.

They may have been busted, but I knew when I was beat.

In the months and years to come, I pretended that our rules were in effect, and Ebby pretended to follow them. By the end of his life with us, Ebby had taught me much. Best of all, I was blessed with the experience—no, the privilege—of receiving his unconditional love. And being the boss wasn't so important anymore.

~Ava Pennington

The Ultimate Designer Dog

You know, if we don't take her, she'll have to go back to the shelter. And who knows what will happen to her." It's a mother's prerogative to use guilt at will, and I was laying it on as thick as country gravy over biscuits. I felt sad and helpless as I waited for a response from my family. I knew we would take my mother's dog even though we didn't want to; it was an obligation I had to impose.

It wasn't that Sallie wasn't a nice dog; she just wasn't the type of dog we would have chosen. After my dad died, my mom had put all her love into Reggie, the dog my parents had together. "He's the only reason I have to get up every morning," she always said. When Reggie died, Mom was devastated. I knew she wouldn't last long without a dog, but I hoped she'd wait until I could get into town to help her find another companion. I imagined a small, cuddly dog

Mom could snuggle with in her favorite chair. Then when the house got too big for her, she could take her laptop companion with her to a retirement home, where they could grow old together.

No such luck. Three days after Reggie died, Mom left me a phone message. "Hi, sweetie. I stopped by the animal shelter today just to look, and guess what? I got a new dog. Her name is Sallie, and she's a one-year-old border collie and greyhound mix. She'd been abused and looked so sad, I just had to take her home.

"She's so cute," Mom gushed. "She has these big ears, and every time I talk to her, she cocks her head to the side and listens so sweetly, just like your dad used to . . . just kidding! Best of all, she's so quiet, I'm not sure she knows how to bark. Can't wait for you to meet her! Love you."

I hung up the phone in disbelief. What in the world was the shelter thinking, matching a seventy-three-year-old woman with a large, energetic dog? I knew I had to talk some sense into her the following weekend. She needed a small dog, one she could easily handle by herself.

At first sight, Sallie is a funny-looking dog. She's black-and-white like a border collie, with the long gangly legs and lean body of a greyhound. She has a slender face, with one brown eye and one ice-blue eye, but it's her ears everyone notices. They are two sizes too big for her body and stand straight up, giving her a perpetual deer-in-the-headlights look.

When I met Sallie for the first time, she came bounding over to me and landed her front paws on my chest, knocking me against the refrigerator. She wouldn't come when called and didn't walk well on a leash. She slobbered all over the floor after drinking water, making walking treacherous in the kitchen. I saw disaster with a capital D. I envisioned Sallie accidentally knocking Mom down the stairs, breaking her arm or her hip or even her head.

"Mom," I gingerly broached the subject, "wouldn't a smaller dog be better for you? One you could hold in your lap? I could take Sallie back for you and see if there's a cute little poodle-type dog that needs a home."

Mom's green eyes steeled a little to let me know I had stepped over the line. "No, dear, I can still make my own decisions," she replied in her no-nonsense, because-I'm-your-mother, that's-why tone. "I don't want a yappy, little frou-frou dog. I picked Sallie because she needed me. Her days were numbered at the shelter, if you know what I mean, and if I hadn't gone when I did, she probably wouldn't be around today. She's a sweet dog, and we've already bonded. Don't worry, dear, we'll be fine. I promise."

And they were fine. Sallie adapted easily to Mom's sedentary lifestyle, and they became inseparable. Sallie was too strong for Mom to walk, but she felt comfortable taking her for daily car rides. When friends visited, Sallie became her guardian, sitting quietly next to her as if listening intently to the conversation. And they were both ready for bed by nine o'clock. It was as if Sallie had turned into an old lady herself. Even children were too loud and rambunctious for her, as my daughter found out when running down the hall once and getting tackled by Sallie. I still thought they were mismatched, but Mom was happy, and that was what mattered.

As hard as my family tried, though, we could not warm up to Sallie. My daughter said she wasn't fun; my husband hated her excessive shedding; and I simply didn't like her looks. She just wasn't a dog for us, and I worried that one day Mom would need us to take her.

Sure enough, four years later, Mom decided to move to a retirement home and wanted us to adopt Sallie. I tried to refuse as gently as possible.

"Mom, we really don't want another dog. Besides, she doesn't like kids and lots of people around. She wouldn't be happy living with us."

I saw the hurt in Mom's eyes as she said it was okay, the shelter could probably find her a new home.

She played the guilt card brilliantly, and I knew I couldn't break her heart. Sallie would be coming home with us.

"Thank you," she said, tears glistening in her eyes. "And don't worry, dear, you'll be fine. I promise."

I waited for my family's reaction to the news as the morning sun peeked through the slatted blinds in the kitchen, as if trying to start our day with a smile. Tom, my husband, was pragmatic about it, but my daughter, Cassie, resisted as only an eleven-year-old can. "We already have a dog, Rosie, remember? And you guys said we can only have two pets in this house, and I've wanted a cat, like, forever, and you promised me one for my birthday. Besides, Sallie doesn't even like me!"

"Cassie, honey, it would be cruel to send her back to the shelter. She had a nice home with Grammy. Sallie will adjust to us quickly, because she knows us. And I promise to take her to obedience school, so she'll be even better behaved than you." My attempt at humor was met with a cold stare and a lower lip jutting out like a facial speed bump.

"We need to do this, sweetie," I pressed on, "for Grammy."

Cassie crossed her arms in resignation, her brown eyes sad, yet defiant. "Well, okay. But I'm changing Sallie's name to Kitty!"

We took Kitty (a.k.a. Sallie) home with us after Christmas that year, and to our surprise, she did adapt well, even to her new name. With Kitty's border collie intelligence, obedience school was a breeze. We were amazed at how fast she learned her commands. Taking Kitty to the park is now fun. She's learned to play, outrunning the other dogs in the dog park with her greyhound speed to catch Frisbees in mid-air. And she seems to thrive on all the extra activity a household of three has compared to Mom's quieter lifestyle.

Best of all, Cassie and Kitty have become good friends. Cassie's a teenager now, and when she gets home from school, Kitty smothers her with sloppy dog kisses. If Cassie is upset over boyfriends or school, she turns not to me but to Kitty. They sit together on the floor in our walk-in bedroom closet (Kitty's "cave") amongst all the clothes and shoes, like two best girlfriends, with Cassie telling Kitty all her deepest secrets, knowing Kitty will keep every one. It's a beautiful friendship Cassie will always treasure.

As for me, I realize now that I, too, had judged Kitty too quickly. She is one of the gentlest, most loving dogs we have ever owned. We thought she would be our albatross, but instead she's been the ultimate "designer" dog—designing her personality to fit first my mom's sedentary life and then our hectic lifestyle.

My mother passed away recently, and one day not long after the funeral, like Cassie, I found solace sitting in the closet with Kitty. There, surrounded by darkness, I cried, feeling the enormous loss of a mother who was also my friend. Kitty sat quietly next to me as if she knew her job was to comfort me. I scratched behind those big ears of hers and gently hugged her. She nuzzled my cheek and then licked my tears as if to say, "Don't worry, we'll be fine." Just like Mom had promised.

~Linda Douglas

Cosmic Changes

When we got a dog twelve years ago, I expected certain things: He'd have an accident or two on the rug. He'd chew a pair of shoes carelessly left within his reach. He'd play tag with my boys in the yard. And, eventually, he would die.

What I didn't expect was that he'd teach my boys to be the men I'd always hoped they would be.

Our dog, Cosmo, died last week, but this isn't a sad, dead dog story. Cosmo wasn't the kind of dog who inspired literature, like Old Yeller or Buck in *The Call of the Wild*. He wasn't made for TV, like Lassie, or even cartoons, like the sleuthing, snacking Scooby Doo. He couldn't even do a stupid pet trick. Cosmo was not extraordinary in any way. He was just a simple family dog who didn't chase squirrels and specialized in naps. Cosmo came into our lives when he was a golden retriever puppy. My sons, seven-year-old Nick and four-year-old Paul had begged for a puppy. I didn't want a dog. I knew how much work dogs were, how hard they were to train, how demanding they were. I had owned dogs before, but my husband never had, and so he was on the boys' side. He extracted promises I knew they would never keep: feed him, bathe him, play with him every day. I knew they would not, could not, be solely responsible for a dog. Although they promised now, later they would refuse to pick up the dog poop in the yard and then complain bitterly when they stepped in a mound. They would grow into teenagers and not have time for him anymore.

Besides the work entailed in caring for a dog, I'm just not a dog person to start with. I don't like panting and drooling. I don't like dogs that jump on me. I don't like the way they insistently stick their noses in my crotch. I've been bitten by dogs, deep enough to draw blood, three times. Dogs are so needy, and the request for a dog came when it felt that the boys and my husband, especially, were suffocating me with their own demands and needs. I didn't want one more thing pulling at me, one more commitment that made me feel locked in.

I remember the night I changed my mind about getting a dog. The boys had been begging again. Nick had already picked out the name—Cosmo, inspired by Carl Sagan. Paul pretended to be Cosmo, frolicking on all fours, chasing whatever Nick threw and bringing it back in his mouth.

When the boys ran off to play elsewhere, my husband hissed, "It's bad enough that we're ruining their lives with our bad marriage, but now we won't let them have a dog, either?"

That night, his words, still stinging, kept me awake. I remembered what it was like having a dog as a teenager—someone to cuddle with and tell my secrets to. Kids need someone who is always happy to see them and never corrects their grammar or tells them to clean up their rooms. They need someone they can play with or just be still with, someone completely devoted to them and with no other job in the world than to celebrate their existence. My boys needed a dog.

I found a reputable golden retriever breeder, and we brought Cosmo into our fractured home. He had an accident on the rug and chewed a pair of shoes, and he chased the boys in the yard with glee. Over the years, I had to remind the boys to feed him and to let him out and then remind them again to let him back in. They complained about stepping in poop that they refused to clean up. It was exactly as I had expected.

When Nick was fifteen and Paul was twelve, my husband and I told them we were getting a divorce. We had already made all the living arrangements, including for the pets. Cosmo would live with their dad, where he would also have a great yard to run and poop in. I would keep the two cats, guinea pig, and fish. The boys would have pets no matter where they were. This accommodation lasted for a year, until the day the boys rushed into my home very upset.

"Dad's getting rid of Cosmo," they wailed.

I had lived a year without the demands of a dog, and, frankly, I had enjoyed it. But seeing how upset the boys were trumped my misgivings. That was how Cosmo returned to my house, coming and going with the boys in accordance to our custody arrangement.

While the boys grew into young men, Cosmo grew into an old man. First he went gray in the muzzle, and then his entire body turned white. He lost the sight in one eye, but with his other one, he still watched squirrels steal food from my bird feeders. He'd sniff out a rabbit trail in the garden but was too tired to chase it down. He slept most of the day, and when awake, he stared vacantly off into space.

Two weeks ago while my younger son, now sixteen, and Cosmo were at my home, Cosmo couldn't get up. My ex-husband came over, lifted him into the back of his SUV, and took him to the vet. With a handful of prescriptions, Cosmo seemed a bit better and stayed the next week with my ex-husband.

My other son, Nick, now nineteen, came home

on leave from the Marine Corps last week, and we were so happy to see him, to have him home and safe. Cosmo, content that his boys were reunited, passed away the next night. Wrapped in a favorite blanket on the kitchen floor, he went in his sleep, as if it were just one more nap to take.

We left it up to the boys whether they wanted to be part of Cosmo's burial. They had never done this before. When the guinea pig died, I alone buried it in the backyard. When one of the cats fell seriously ill, the vet euthanized her and disposed of her body. The fish seemed to just disappear on their own. This time, there was no question in Nick's mind: he would go along to bury Cosmo. Paul followed his brother's lead. They were ready with shovels when their father arrived. I cut flowers from the yard where Cosmo had chased his boys, and I tied the bouquet with ribbons.

Cosmo lay wrapped in his blanket in the back of the SUV. I pulled back the blanket and patted the gray fur of his cheek. "You're a good dog, Cosmo, such a sweet puppy," I said, as I always did to him, even long after his puppy days were over. I replaced the blanket and placed the flowers on top. The boys flanked me and put their arms around me as I cried, then they climbed in the SUV and drove away to bury their dog.

I didn't go with them, although I could have. It didn't seem right for me to go. I had never wanted Cosmo, not initially, nor after his return to my house after the divorce. I let him go, just as I had accepted him—from a distance.

The boys were quiet when they returned home. Nick played a video game on the computer, while Paul lay on his bed staring at the ceiling.

"How did it go?" I asked.

Paul stretched and worked his feet against imaginary pedals. Nick took aim at animated aliens and efficiently destroyed them. I waited. Finally Nick said, "It was pretty emotional."

At my ex-husband's vineyard, they'd dug a hole on the hill overlooking the lake in a patch of wildflowers where Cosmo liked to roll. They'd laid him in the hole and covered him over with dirt. They'd piled rocks into the shape of a pine tree as a headstone and placed the flowers from my yard on the grave. Then they all, father and sons, had cried together.

"It's the first time I've cried in years," Paul said, his wild mop of hair spread out around him on the pillow. "It was hard."

The boys were quiet, and I told them that I was proud of them, that Cosmo sure loved them, that he was a good dog. They nodded, because there was nothing more to say and they knew all I'd said was true.

I don't know that Cosmo prevented my boys' lives from being ruined by our lousy marriage; I think that's too much to ask of a dog, especially one with such a penchant for napping. I don't know if the boys ever whispered their secrets in his ear or whether he was ever a comfort to them in moments of sadness. He was just an ordinary dog who was always happy to see them, a consistent welcome in their inconsistent lives.

My boys are no longer boys. They have grown into men, and Cosmo, in his final act, let them prove that. A child would have let his father dispose of a dead pet on his own, but a man would stand up and do the right thing, even if it were unpleasant or difficult. Cosmo's surprising final gift was to show me what fine young men my sons have become in spite of the choices their father and I made that might have ruined their lives.

I don't miss the dog hair that floated like tumbleweeds along the floor, and I won't miss dodging poop in the yard. But I find myself missing Cosmo more than I thought I would. He always had a knowing look in his eyes, but I could never figure out what he was trying to tell me. I think I know now. He was trying to say it would be all right and not to worry so much. Everything, everyone would turn out fine.

~Gretchen Stahlman

Ginger, Come Home

My husband, Larry, sat with head in hands, eyes red with unshed tears. Ginger our five-year-old collie, had been spooked when she'd been left outside in the fenced yard during a thunderstorm while we were out of town. Apparently, she had climbed on the roof of her doghouse and bolted over the fence from there.

The teenage boy whom we had trusted to feed her and let her out in the yard daily for exercise had decided not to call the emergency number we'd left to tell us she was missing. So we didn't find out until a week later, when we returned home. His reasoning was that he didn't want to "ruin our vacation." That meant a seven-day delay in looking for a scared collie who had never been free to roam the neighborhood and who had been coddled and cared for since she was born. How would she ever find her way home?

Larry was especially fond of Gingerbread because she was an emotional link to comfort he had found in his less-than-ideal childhood. As a youngster, he had been abandoned by his parents and sent with his two older brothers to another state to live with family friends. Four years later, at age eight, he was separated from his two brothers and shipped off alone to live with complete strangers. He had been frightened and lonely until, at the home he'd shared with his brothers, he'd made friends with a collie named Cookie. Cookie, in turn, gave birth to Crumb. He loved them completely and hated to leave them. When he was permanently adopted at the age of eight, his adoptive parents bought him a collie of his own, which he named Ginger, for the color of her fur. The dogs had each supplied that dose of unconditional love and feeling of belonging Larry needed.

Shortly after we married, I presented Larry on his birthday with a collie pup we named Gingerbread, after his childhood pet. She instantly became a central part of our family. Naturally, when we'd returned home from vacation to find her missing, we felt shock and sorrow, but we also had hope of finding her.

We did what we knew how to do: tacked posters to trees, put an ad in the paper, scoured the

neighborhood, and called the animal shelter daily—
all to no avail. After exhausting our limited leads
and options for finding her, we began to accept her
loss and grieved for her. Our nightly prayers of finding her gradually turned to prayers for her safety and
protection.

We talked of buying another dog but decided
against it, needing time to heal before investing emo-
tionally in another pet. Secretly, we each took note
of every dog running by in the neighborhood and
every dog walked on a leash in the park. We couldn't
quite stop reading the lost-and-found-pet section of
the newspaper. Finally, grieving, but determined to
move forward, we resumed our daily routine, but
with a hole in hearts where Ginger had been.

Approximately six months later, Larry had
another shock when the company where he'd been
employed for a long while suddenly folded. He
scoured the papers, but there were few available posi-
tions in his field in our immediate area. Discouraged,
he finally arranged an interview with a company
about thirty miles from our home, in an area we had
never been to before. Driving the twisted back roads,
he wondered why he had agreed to an interview so
far from home and in such a remote location. *I might
as well turn around and head home,* he thought to
himself as the road stretched out before him. *There*

is no way I'm working out in this wilderness. Still, he pressed forward, determined to follow through with the interview, since he had made the appointment and it would have been irresponsible not to show up.

Arriving in front of the small commercial building, Larry got out of his truck and surveyed his surroundings before approaching the door. As he walked, he noticed a movement near the rear of the building. Was it an animal? Woods loomed on all sides. As he watched, a mangy-looking critter approached him slowly, limping as it came. Larry reached into the back of his truck for a length of pipe for protection, thinking it might be a rabid wolf.

"Easy, boy," he said soothingly. "Easy there." The animal, thin, dirty, and straggly, seemed to wiggle a bit as he spoke. Was it wagging its tail? "Come here, boy," Larry called carefully. "Are you okay?"

The poor creature approached very slowly, head down in the submissive pose of a frightened animal, belly almost dragging the ground, but it was nonetheless wagging a thin rope of a tail. The foul odor emanating from the animal testified to its long time unattended.

Larry adjusted his glasses and looked closely as the wretched "wolf" approached. It was no wolf; it was a dog—one that might have been gingerbread brown and white and lovely. Staring with disbelief, Larry called out a name he had not said in months. "Gingerbread?"

The filthy little bundle lifted her ears and walked faster toward him.

"Ginger?" he asked again.

Reaching down, he took hold of her dirty red collar with an expired rabies vaccination tag. He could not believe his eyes. Grabbing the dog on the sides of her face, Larry examined her closely. A smile broke out from ear to ear, and unshed tears came to his eyes. After six months of searching, here in this remote area outside Houston, at an interview for a job he didn't really want, was his beloved friend, Ginger.

We took Ginger to a vet, who said she had apparently been foraging for herself all that time, that she had probably been struck by a car, given the damage to her leg, but that in spite of everything, she was in remarkably good health.

We don't know what forces came together to bring Ginger and Larry to that unlikely place at the same time, but we were grateful that our collie, Ginger, like the fabled Lassie, had at last come home.

~Susan Mayer Davis

The Sweet Days of Autumn

The wooden handle has lost its shellac, but the timeworn brush and I are partners—both in it for the long haul, for the sake of a graying best friend named Kodie. I could've bought a new brush, but it would have somehow diminished the sacredness of grooming Kodie—like taking the patina off an antique. We're all just too well acquainted by now.

I groom his shoulders with respect. Kodie is massively built. With such bulk, what stranger would guess he's so infinitely gentle? I trace one shoulder with the faithful brush—or maybe it does the work and simply draws my hand along with it; who can tell? It's a small matter, and the only real issue is the appreciative *thud thud thud* of Kodie's hind leg, going through the motions of scratching, because it feels good to be groomed where he can't quite reach any more.

His age makes the reach tougher. Being nearly fourteen years old puts him on the verge of *ancient* for a dog classified as a giant breed. The magic of puppy breath has given way to maturity and then to advancing age. It happened one magical day at a time, so gently and seamlessly it was hard to notice at first.

While Kodie was growing up, his world expanded with each new adventurous day. Now, in his twilight years, his world grows smaller.

The ever-watchful sentinel has discovered the pleasure of naps on a sheepskin in the living room. Now it's only his dreams that carry him to the ridge top, where once he kept watch over his domain. If the sleep is deep enough, he may or may not notice the UPS truck in the driveway or footsteps on the porch.

There is a certain amount of fair wear and tear to being a 140-pound canine. A toll is taken, and joints break down. Pain has become a part of life, and medication to ease it is a daily ritual. Kodie has the wisdom to know when it's hidden in his breakfast—and the grace to eat it anyway, especially when there's a hot dog in the bargain.

Perhaps it's the canine equivalent of retirement. He's napping, he's pausing, and he's found pleasure in quieter things he used to rush headlong past. Aloof in his prime, Kodie now enjoys every scratch behind his ears. It's taken the tinge of silver on his cheeks for him to slow down enough to let me cradle his massive, graying face in my hands.

His eyes, though, have changed little. I search their gentle depths. Some days I see age and pain, some days youthful joy. Every day I see love. The same love of the puppy who chose me. In the midst of a tumble of chubby puppies, I stood confused— they were all wonderful for different reasons. But Kodie already knew. He wagged his whole chunky self up to me, looked into my eyes, and resolutely plopped his not-so-little fanny onto my foot and sat there, his broad puppy face smiling up at me. His puppy-sized attention span was short, and soon he was off to romp with his littermates. He kept coming back to perch on my foot, though, because he knew. He'd chosen me and made himself mine.

And for approaching fourteen years, I have been his.

Kodie has loped endless miles alongside my horse, my constant companion on trail rides. I love the deep woods, with the lighter stretches of dappled sunlight. But when it became hard for him to go along, I came to love those distant rides less. Though his joints were disintegrating, he wouldn't let the pain keep him from scaling the ridge. He did it to be with me, to watch over me. I tried tying him to the porch post at home to save him from himself. When his eyes searched mine for reasons, I didn't have any good enough. So, instead, I stayed with him and rode on familiar turf. And he watched over me. And I watched over him.

I watch over him because Kodie and I have reached that season in our lives. When the time comes for our loving pets to face the final leg of their race, it is up to us to help them finish well.

How do we do that? . . .

We sense the unspoken needs of the companions we know so well. If they seem confused for no reason, we reassure them with a loving touch. We groom them faithfully, but more gently, because the aged, arthritic bones aren't so well padded now. We slow down for their sake, let them enjoy a scent on the wind and to follow a visitor's trail across the yard.

We expect inconveniences, and we don't get angry when they come. We don't let new aches and pains go untreated; we ease what we can. We watch for changes in vision and hearing, and protect those precious senses as long as possible. We care for their teeth, and make food easy to chew. We take them for potty walks before they ask, as it gets easier for them to forget.

We scratch those soft graying ears and go for some of the best car rides ever. If our companions need comfort, we give it freely. If age and infirmity bring a sense of vulnerability, then we step in to protect our old guardians. We watch over them in their deepest slumbers, when dreams take them running across long forgotten fields, and we remember those fields too.

If they are not able to stand alone, we lift them. If their steps become uncertain, we steady them. If their health fails profoundly, it falls on us to ease them to their final rest.

But until that difficult choice is the only course left to us, we savor the moments we have with our companions. We see their old age as a passage, not as a disease or a burden. We accept it as merely another stage of life and welcome the changes it brings.

We let the autumn sun warm our old friend's bones, and ours. We realize that autumn is not a bad time of year at all. It is a beautiful season, the season of harvest. And sometimes the harvest is love.

~Christy Caballero

Big Ole' Mix-Up Dog

We have a big dog. A big, stupid dog. To be precise, we have a big, clumsy, operating-on-only-a-brainstem kind of dog. His name is Copper.

Cop is a mix-up dog. The pet shop said he was a Lab mixed with something. They couldn't determine what he was mixed with. Many others have tried to identify him since then. Some vets have said he was chow, due to the black spots on his big ole' tongue. Others have said that, with his barrel chest and big ole' head, he must have rottweiler in him. One person even agreed with my husband, saying he was definitely half African lion dog. He's got a mix-up look to him, that's for sure. He's big with a huge, square head, a tongue that lolls out when he's happy, a ridge of hair that stands up funny on his backbone, and a Barney-the-dinosaur smile. Whatever he is, he's undeniably special.

Some of Copper's specialness might better be described as strangeness. It all started with Cop's love affair with rocks. He digs them up and carries them around on our three-mile hikes. He lays his tongue across them when he lounges in the backyard. He has redesigned my folks' rock walkway by dragging huge rocks from one spot to another. He even chews up lava rocks like bubble gum! Not the smartest thing to do, but it seems to be his hobby.

Oh, we often joke that Copper's all brawn and very little brain. He has done many mixed-up things that would make most people want to get rid of him. For starters, he created his own doggy door by crashing through the bottom of the storm door that shut just a fraction of a second too soon. He's eaten whole loaves of bread that were left on the counter. He's even eaten whole Lego creations without our knowledge. (We only found out when we scooped up the remains in the backyard.) He's knocked over tables, chewed through lamp cords that luckily weren't plugged in, and worn a racetrack in the backyard lawn. He's even attacked a huge cement raccoon lawn ornament that he thought was real! Nothing seems to slow him down.

One day we were playing fetch with him in the

field behind our house. We didn't know it then, but there was a barbed-wire fence covered by tall field grass running through a part of the area and Copper found it. He was running full speed to get the tennis ball and suddenly seemed to slam into something. He bounced backward and then tilted his head a bit, as though inspecting something in the grass. He then darted off in pursuit of the ball, bringing it back to us all wags and doggy-drool smiles. We continued the game for a few more tosses before we noticed that his right front leg was wet. It was bloody. I leaned down close to him and could see the gash in his leg, a flap of fur exposing muscle underneath. And Copper still wanted to play!

We laugh now and say that his having no pain receptors made it easy for the vet to administer the four staples that day. Cop just laid there and watched the vet work. He didn't even flinch! He didn't follow the vet's post-op orders very closely, either. He wanted to play the minute he got off the operating table. You gotta love a mix-up dog like that.

What really makes us love him, though, is his steadfast loyalty. Oh, we joke a ton that he's not the sharpest tool in the shed. But we know there's no other dog we'd rather have by our side than this mix-up dog.

My sister agrees. She was on a hike in the hills

near our family's old homestead. With her was "the pack"—her cockapoo, our folks' German shepherd, our other much smaller dog, and Copper. Well, to make a long story short, my sister fell. She landed on her back in the gravel amidst the pine trees far from the house. All the dogs kept walking. That is, all of them except Cop. He alone turned around when he realized she wasn't with them any longer. He walked back to her and lay down beside her. He licked her face. She put her hand across his broad back and used him to pull herself up to her feet again. When she was steady and brushed off, Copper stood up beside her. Then they walked back to the house together. He stopped only momentarily to pick up a big rock, which he carried with him.

That's it in a nutshell, really: *He* walked *her.* He walks us all. We don't walk him. Oh, we think we do. We carry the leash and all. We pet him and feel like we're doing him a favor by taking him out. But that's not it. Copper takes us. He takes us by the heartstrings and leads us through the walk. And not just one walk. Every walk, every single day, Copper takes us and protects us and makes sure we get home safely.

Yes, we have a big dog. A big ole' mix-up dog. We love him so.

~Kristine Downs

Dogs Eat Bread?

U nlike most dogs, Carly, a sheltie/shepherd mix, did not gobble up every speck of food put in front of her. She would take the offered item politely, put it on the floor, and sniff it. Then she would turn her apologetic gaze to me as if to say, "What, exactly, do you expect me to do with this?"

She certainly never ate plain bread. Carly understood she was a dog, and simple dog food would do. But one day on a visit to my Italian grandmother, she proved she understood much more than that.

I grew up next door to my grandparents' house, and there, dogs lived outside, were all named Shep, and ate leftover bread and spaghetti sauce for supper. By the time I was in my twenties and had adopted Carly, the Sheps were long gone, and when we visited, my grandparents allowed my dog inside.

In the kitchen, I sat at the table, fascinated, while

Grandma shuffled back and forth in her faded flowered dress and stained apron, getting food for me—as if I could eat six different kinds of cold cuts, half a loaf of Italian bread, a thick slice of fried eggplant, spaghetti and meatballs, salad, and cheesecake all by myself at three o'clock in the afternoon.

Carly trailed after Grandma's ratty Keds—the comfy ones with the toes cut out of them—as she performed her everyday magic of producing a banquet on a moment's notice. "*Mangia,*" Grandma said as she moved from refrigerator to cabinet to pantry and back, placing another item on the table each time she passed. "You want some cheese?"

"No thanks, Grandma, really. This is plenty."

She put the full round of mozzarella in front of me anyway, just in case.

"You're too skinny."

"Why don't you sit down with me?" I asked.

Grandma continued to bustle around her kitchen, her every step literally dogged by a furry girl eagerly seeking yummy morsels. *That's my dog?* I thought. *My courteous and respectful Carly?* She never followed me around the kitchen like that. She never followed anyone like that, and she never begged for people food.

I picked at the love offering Grandma had lain on the table. The right thing to do was to *mangia* with gusto, but I wasn't hungry, not that it mattered.

This was Grandma's way of showing she cared. To reciprocate, I should eat.

She eyed me from her station by the stove and gestured in my direction with a spoon. "You got a boyfriend?"

Here we go. "Yes," I answered, "but he's not Italian."

She emitted an eloquent, long-suffering sigh and returned to stirring the pot, but not without noticing Carly at her feet.

"Carly, here," I said. "Get out of Grandma's way."

"Eh," Grandma dismissed me with a wave of her hand. I was too skinny, lacked the sense to eat, and had a non-Italian boyfriend. I was not worth talking to, especially since I had not brought said non-Italian boyfriend around so she could squeeze his cheeks between her hands and see for herself whether he was Italian.

My dog, on the other hand, showed more interest in Grandma's food than I did. She glanced down into Carly's brown eyes. "What do want, eh? You want a piece of bread?"

Carly's tail thumped the floor.

I cut a piece of bread for myself. "She won't eat it," I said as I folded a few slices of prosciutto into the stiff curl of the crusty homemade loaf. Carly licked her chops, her eyes following Grandma's every move, as if a bite of medium-rare sirloin might fall out of her apron pocket. Grandma leaned over the table, tore off a hunk of bread, and offered it to Carly. Carly, in her gentle way, took it and ate it. I stopped chewing, narrowed my eyes at my dog, and watched her throat work the dry treat down to her tummy.

Grandma nodded in approval. Carly looked as if she might like another taste of that delicious, plain bread. I slumped in my chair, at first surprised, then astonished, as she accepted and ate another piece. She continued to shadow the old woman over the cracked linoleum floor. *This is a trick,* I thought.

Grandma, validated in her dogs-eat-bread belief system, lowered herself into a chair, oblivious to the miracle she had wrought. She rested her chin against her palm and fixed her bright eyes on me.

"You should shop around," she said, getting back to the important matter of men.

"So you've said," I answered absently, not meaning to be rude, but still in shock. I kept my gaze on Carly, waiting for what, I didn't know. At that point, she could have recited The Declaration of Independence, and I wouldn't have been surprised. The dog shoved her damp nose under my hand. I stroked her silky ears.

"Find a man with money," my grandmother continued with a wagging finger. "But a man who's had to work for it."

I'd heard this advice before and knew it contained wisdom. But the mystery of Grandma and Carly and the bread had me confounded, so I could not engage in the other philosophical issue. I was still pondering what had happened. *What enlightenment, beyond fundamental civility, had my dog demonstrated? What alchemy had my grandmother wrought before my eyes? Was the power of her belief so strong that she bent my non-bread-eating dog to her will without thought?* Beneath my hand, Carly shrugged, as if wondering what my mental fussing was about. Had she known in the queer way dogs know things that she should eat whatever this old woman offered simply because it was the right thing to do? I'll never know, but I like contemplating the possibilities. Perhaps there was a lesson there for me—that anything is possible with love.

I do know Grandma was right about shopping for a man. It took a while, but I found a good one, and we married. He had the privilege of being kissed by Carly but not of having his cheeks squeezed by my Italian grandmother. And Carly, who had never eaten bread before that day at Grandma's, never ate bread again, no matter how much I learned or believed, and no matter how often I begged.

~Candace Carrabus

Away, Sam

The sweet, green hills of New Zealand are covered with sheep, a constant restless tide always on the lookout for another blade of grass. When it's time to shift to another pasture and the shepherd whistles the dogs to work, the sheep move like a river, flowing steadily toward the gate. A sharp whistle and the shepherd's voice float across the grassy space. Flashes of black and brown change the flow as the shepherd directs his dogs in an age-old rhythm.

My husband and I managed a farm with three-thousand ewes, and I longed to be able to tread the hills with my own dogs, sending them out in perfect harmony to move the big mobs of sheep. I wanted to be useful, which to me meant being able to move sheep from pasture to pasture. When I'd try with my husband's dogs, they'd look at me with disdain and then head off to chase rabbits, leaving me to race after the sheep myself. They acted as though working for me was one step above a bath.

Sam came to me in his semi-retirement years. He was about ten years old and had worked faithfully for my husband's uncle. Uncle Jack maintained that Sam secretly wanted to be owned by a woman, having been raised by a farmer's wife. He figured the best place for Sam to spend his golden years was working for someone with a soft voice and gentle hands. At last, here was a dog that wanted to work with me and ignored my husband.

Sam's breeding made him a "handy" dog—a uniquely New Zealand cross between a loud, rollicking "huntaway" and a silent, stealthy "heading" dog. The huntaway works at the back of the mob, barking loudly and often. Sheep have no natural predators in New Zealand and need to be pushed to make them move. The heading dog turns or stops the mob by gliding to the front and staring down the lead sheep. If the mating to create a handy dog works, you get a dog that barks at the back and then races to the front to silently turn the mob. If it doesn't work, you get a mess, a dog that barks at all the wrong times, scattering the sheep like BBs and turning them when they should go straight ahead.

Sam turned out to be one of the useful handy dogs. He was of medium build and had short black-and-tan fur, pointy ears, calm eyes, and a long tail. His whole body wagged when I pulled on my boots, his signal that we'd either be working or going for a walk.

When he wasn't moving sheep, Sam would snooze peacefully under the big tree in front of our house. Once, he went to pet day at the school with one of our sons, where he won a prize in the dress-up class as a trusty sidekick to our cowboy-togged boy. Sam did look sideways at me that day when I gave him a bath beforehand. Working dogs, even semi-retired ones, never appreciate personal hygiene.

Sam and I worked the small mobs, manageable for an old dog and his novice handler. I learned to read him and the sheep, and eventually we got our timing in sync. It was such freedom to call out, "Away, Sam," and send him to just the right place to successfully move groups of fifty to 100 sheep around the farm. Sam and I were a team of two, and I felt handy in my own way.

I knew Sam's retirement day would eventually come, when even the small mobs would be too much. But dogs don't do retirement timelines nor let their handlers in on their plans.

One day, we headed out to move some sheep down the road, with the woolshed the final destination. The shed was about half a hour away and involved a trek down a paved road. That road made a sharp turn at the bottom of the hill, but the sheep needed to go straight ahead into a dirt road. If we messed up at that corner, the sheep continued toward a one-lane bridge and a neighbor's front lawn and lovingly tended flowers.

I stood at the top of the hill, ready to send Sam to the front of the mob. "Away, Sam," I sang out, expecting to see him flashing through the long grass at the side of the road. Sam remained by my side, looking into the distance. "Away, Sam," I said again, a bit more firmly. He licked my hand, then sat. Clearly, he was not going to be the one to turn the sheep, which were now streaming down the road and gathering momentum with the slope. With an unladylike oath and hoping that he wasn't sick, I ran off through the pasture beside the road, vaulting over gates and stumbling onto the road in front of the sheep just as they rounded the corner. They stopped, surprised to see me instead of the usual black and tan flash barking at them. I managed a few weak gasps, and they turned obediently toward the dirt road. Looking around, I saw Sam trotting happily through the pasture, stopping now and then to sniff around and roll in the long grass. He caught up with me, staying by my side as the sheep walked down the road. They ended up in the right place with no help or encouragement from him.

As I watched Sam keep pace with me, all the frustration drained away. He knew the time was here. After three years, Sam had announced his retirement without any fanfare, parties, or gold watches. I hope I'm as decisive as Sam when my big life decisions come along.

He never herded another sheep, though he always came to watch. We walked around the farm, doing jobs that didn't involve herding, enjoying his last years. I never minded if he wanted to stop and smell the clover. We'd stop together and sit on the side of a hill, watching the other dogs work. Sometimes we'd just stand and stare into the distance. You can see a long way if you look with a calm eye.

We buried Sam when he was thirteen, under his snoozing tree. All the dogs I've had since have benefited from the lessons he taught me when I called out, "Away, Sam."

~Kathryn Godsiff

Contributors

Beth Rothstein Ambler ("Butkus on Guard" and "Clod of My Heart") recently relocated from New Jersey to Colorado, where she lives with her husband, Chuck, and her constant source of writing inspiration, Syco. She began writing when she left her management career after a diagnosis of multiple sclerosis.

Carolyn Blankenship ("Trouble on the Hoof"), of Austin, Texas, teaches classes on creativity, memoir, and journal writing. She is the program director for the board of Story Circle Network and the author of *From the Heart: A Manual for Facilitators*. She delights in gardening, grandkids, and traveling with her husband, Monty.

Sharyn L. Bolton ("The Escape Artist"), of Mill Creek, Washington, was a psychologist, an account sales manager, and the head of a consulting firm specializing in custom-designed training programs before she became a freelance writer. Her articles, short stories, and essays have appeared in regional and national publications.

Christy Caballero ("The Sweet Days of Autumn") is a freelance writer who lives a few deer trails off the beaten path in rural Oregon. She has received journalism awards through the National Federation of Press Women, and the Dog Writers Association of America honored her with a Maxwell Award for her work on Vietnam War dogs. She practices and writes about Reiki for animals.

Priscilla Carr ("The Major") lives with her husband, Richard, in Nottingham, New Hampshire. She was the 2006 Writer in Residence at the Artcroft Creative Center in Kentucky. A poet, memoirist, and freelance journalist, she has been published in *Northern New England Review* and is working on a memoir of Jane Kenyon.

Candace Carrabus ("Dogs Eat Bread?") is a technical writer and Web site designer, when she isn't writing stories. She lives on a farm outside St. Louis with her architect husband, wonderful daughter, nine cats, two horses, and two dogs—both of whom love bread, but only if it is topped with spaghetti sauce.

Loy Michael Cerf ("The Anti-Alpha Male") is an animal-loving, Chicago-area freelance writer. She enjoys crocheting blankets for Project Linus and dreaming up creative ways to coerce her grown children into petsitting, so she can guiltlessly cruise the globe with her husband of thirty-something years.

Lisa Ricard Claro ("Sandy Dreams") is a freelance writer of personal essays and fiction in every genre. Her work often appears in the *Atlanta-Journal Constitution,* and she is seeking to publish a novel. Her loves include her husband, children, two spoiled cats, and a rambunctious yellow Labrador puppy named Rigby.

Sue Dallman-Carrizales ("Hope in a Dumpster") was born and raised in Madison, Wisconsin, and moved to Colorado after earning a master's degree in social work in 1988. Now a policy specialist with the state of Colorado, she lives in Denver with her husband, two Labradors, and a white cat.

Tish Davidson ("Where the Need Is Greatest") is a medical writer specializing in making technical information accessible to people outside the health care community. She is also the author of many parenting articles as well as six nonfiction books. She lives in Fremont, California, and is a volunteer puppy raiser for Guide Dogs for the Blind.

Amy Rose Davis ("Born to Be Wild") and her husband, Bryce, live in Gresham, Oregon, with their four children. Amy works as a freelance business copywriter and ghostwriter, and her work has appeared in *A Cup of Comfort® for Mothers to Be*, *A Cup of Comfort® for Writers*, *Northwest Construction* magazine, and the *Oregon Humane Society* magazine.

Susan Mayer Davis ("Ginger, Come Home") is a writer and editor for a nonprofit organization. At home, she divides her leisure time between writing, reading, and oil painting. An award-winning fiction writer, she is currently working on her first novel. Susan lives in Snellville, Georgia, with her family and their rescued Lab, Abby.

Marla Doherty ("Bellatrix"), who remembers Bell with love and undying gratitude, lives with her husband, Chuck, and their daughter, Malina, in Redding, California. She and her family enjoy biking, hiking, camping, and snow-skiing. Lately, Daisy, their thirteen-year-old Brittany spaniel/Lab pup, prefers naps and leisurely strolls over the family's more strenuous activities.

Linda Douglas ("The Ultimate Designer Dog") lives in Edwardsville, Illinois, with her husband, daughter, and two dogs. She has been published in *Writers' Journal* and several online magazines. She is also a trained volunteer with Noah's Wish, a national organization dedicated to rescuing animals during disasters.

Kristine Downs ("Big Ole' Mix-Up Dog") is a lifelong writer living in Rapid City, South Dakota. Her husband,

Dave, and son, Max, provide a test audience for her essays, novels, poems, and plays. She shares her love of writing every day, teaching elementary school students to put thought on paper.

Karin Fuller ("Some Kind of Wonderful") lives in Poca, West Virginia, with her husband, Geoff, and her daughter, Celeste. Along with Furry Murry, they have another only slightly more intelligent dog, and three cats.

Marilyn A. Gelman ("Strange Bedfellows") promotes public awareness of mild traumatic brain injury and advocates for the civil rights of individuals with invisible disabilities. Her publication credits include *The New York Times, Modern Romances, Creative Nonfiction,* and *The Paterson Literary Review.* She lives in northern New Jersey.

Kathleen Gerard ("The Gift That Keeps Giving") lives in New Jersey. Her writing has appeared in various literary journals and anthologies. She is the author of *Still Life,* a spiritual memoir, and her work has been nominated for *Best New American Voices,* a national prize in literature.

Kathryn Godsiff ("Away, Sam") and her husband, Allan, raised three boys and many sheep during eighteen years in New Zealand. She now lives in the central Oregon town of Sisters, where she and Allan manage a small ranch. She writes for a regional horse magazine and spends her free time trail-riding.

Ginny Greene ("Ditto, Darling") still loves her home state of Washington, but for the past ten years her heart has been tethered near Abilene, Texas. During that time, she has herded goat kids and grandkids and has written the monthly newsletter for the Abilene Writers Guild, for which she currently resides as president.

Cathy C. Hall ("The Cost of a Dog"), of Lilburn, Georgia, is a humor columnist for a regional magazine. She writes about her husband, three children, and of course, Sally, the wonder dog. But only Sally thinks she's funny.

Ellen D. Hosafros ("Puzzle") is a former award-winning newspaper columnist, feature writer, and editor. She currently manages a marketing services department for a manufacturer in Grand Rapids, Michigan. She and her husband, Edward, are the parents of two grown sons. She recently completed her first novel, *Mental*, and is writing another.

Dennis Jamison ("For the Love of a Dog") works as a customer correspondence specialist with a medical device manufacturer. His writing has been published in local newspapers as well as in *A Cup of Comfort® for Grandparents*. He lives in the San Francisco Bay Area with his wife and youngest son, and he truly misses his two older children, who are attending Southern California colleges.

Marsha Mott Jordan ("If He Only Had a Brain") created the Hugs and Hope Foundation for Critically Ill Children and is the author of *Hugs, Hope, and Peanut Butter*, the profits of which all go to sick children. Her writing has been published in several magazines, including *Heartlight, Obadiah*, and *Christian Voices*. King Louie allows Marsha and her rocket scientist husband to share their home with him in Wisconsin.

Brenda Kezar ("Beauty in the Beast") is a writer and home-schooling mom in North Dakota. She and her husband have two daughters and share their home with two dogs, several cats, and an assortment of small animals. Between hairballs, she writes every chance she gets. Her work also appears in *A Cup of Comfort® for Writers*.

Lyndell King ("Bloodlines and Heartstrings") is a contemporary romance writer from Tasmania, Australia. She also writes for By Grace e-publishing. Her romantic suspense novel, *Come to Heal*, which has won several competitions, is currently being considered by Medallion Press. It will be released under her pen name, Babe King.

Sue Lamoree ("My Saving Grace") lives in Seattle, Washington, with her husband, her dog, Cinder, and a very large cat. After retiring from her career in finance, she now enjoys writing, horseback riding, and playing with Cinder. Her stories have appeared in *Horse Crazy* and *The Healing Touch of Horses* under the name Sue Hutchinson.

Susan Luzader ("Doggie Do-Si-Do") lives in Tucson, Arizona, with her husband, Randy, and two cattle dogs, Duchess and Leo. A charter member of the Fabulous Women Writing Group, she conducts workshops to help other writers build confidence and skills.

Allison Maher ("The Tail of a Chesapeake") lives on a fruit farm in Nova Scotia, Canada, with her two children and husband, David Bowlby. She writes articles for newspapers and magazines. Her first novel, *I, The Spy*, was published in spring 2006.

Hope Irvin Marston ("Comrades") is a retired junior high librarian and an awarding-winning author of two dozen children's books and two adult titles. She lives with her husband and their Bernese mountain dog in upstate New York. Her first novel for young adults, *Margaret of the Killing Times*, was recently released.

Julie Matherly ("The Human Whisperer") is a writer living in Florida with her husband and magical dog. She was the first-place romance novel winner in the 2005 Southwest Writers competition and essay winner in the 2005 Yosemite Writers Conference contest. She's also written a novel about the empowerment that can come from overcoming grief.

Lad Moore ("A Leave from Absence") enjoys hundreds of publishing credits and has earned several writing awards, including a nomination to the Texas Institute of Letters. His short stories have been published in several anthologies, including *A Cup of Comfort*® and *Chicken Soup for the Soul*, and two collections of his works are available through major booksellers. He resides in the historic steamboat town of Jefferson, Texas.

Lori M. Myers ("Free Willy"), of Harrisburg, Pennsylvania, is an award-winning freelance writer with more than 700 articles, essays, and short fiction published in more than forty national and regional publications. She is the cofounder of the Central Pennsylvania Writers' Consortium and teaches writing workshops in the region.

Ava Pennington ("Who's the Boss?") resides in Stuart, Florida, with her husband, Russ. She holds an MBA from St. John's University and is a graduate of Moody Bible Institute. A former human resources director, she spends her time teaching Bible studies, writing, and public speaking. Her articles and stories have appeared in magazines and anthologies.

Marion Roach ("Dogs Who Do Things") is the author of *The Roots of Desire: The Myth, Meaning, and Sexual Power of Red Hair* (Bloomsbury), coauthor of *Dead Reckoning* (Simon & Schuster), and the author of *Another Name for Madness* (Houghton Mifflin). She lives in upstate New York with her family.

Julie Clark Robinson ("My Black-and-White Wonder") is the author of *Live in the Moment*. Her work has appeared in *Family Circle* and several volumes of *A Cup of Comfort*®, and her column appears on several women's motivational Web sites. She lives in Hudson, Ohio, with her husband, two children, and their black Lab, Pal.

Robert Rohloff ("Sonata for Bach"), a native of Nebraska who now resides in Canada, is a gourmet chef by trade. As a young man, he hitchhiked across Canada and most of the United States, an experience that taught him much about human nature. He credits his Bohemian ancestry for his gypsy soul and way of life.

Marcia Rudoff ("The Rent Collector") teaches memoir writing at the Bainbridge Island Senior Center (Washington State) and is a newspaper columnist for the *Bainbridge Review*. Her personal essays have appeared in *Stories with Grace, Northwest Runner, The Seattle Times,* and several anthologies, including *A Cup of Comfort® for Inspiration, Rocking Chair Reader, Horse Crazy,* and *Classic Christmas.*

Gail Sattler ("Green Roof, Red Car, Dog on Roof") resides in Vancouver, British Columbia, Canada, where she writes (quietly), plays the bass guitar (loudly), and doesn't have to shovel rain. She is the award-winning author of more than thirty books; the mother of three children; and the keeper of two schnauzers, one lizard, two toads, and a multitude of tropical fish, many of which have names.

Laurie Alice Skonicki-Eakes ("Blind Trust") is a full-time writer, whose publishing credits include one hardcover and two paperback novels as well as numerous articles and essays. Although she no longer runs, she loves to walk, read, and enjoy good conversation. She lives in northern Virginia with her husband and sundry animals.

Tanya Sousa ("Sisters") is a guidance counselor and writer living in Barton, Vermont. She writes for *Dog and Kennel, The Canine Chronicle,* and other dog magazines, and is the author of the how-to book *Can Dogs Read? Starting and Implementing a Literacy Program* (Cairn Terrier Publishing).

Gretchen Stahlman ("Cosmic Changes") is an award-winning technical writer in upstate New York. Beyond her left-brain work, she uses her right brain to write personal essays, columns, a memoir, a blog, and currently, a novel.

Using both sides of her brain keeps her from wobbling so she won't fall down.

Emily Alexander Strong ("A Heeling Heart") divides her time between writing and raising her two young daughters, Eliza and Harper. Always the fair mom, she has published a story about each of them in *It's a Girl* and *A Cup of Comfort® for Mothers-to-Be*. She resides with her husband, Eric, and daughters in Ashland, Oregon.

Amy Walton ("A Gift Returned"), of Virginia Beach, Virginia, is the single mother of two sons, an army officer and a high school soccer player. She's also the proud "mom" of a slightly overweight Dalmatian, who has stolen her heart. When not giving him belly rubs or taking him on long walks, she is a museum educator, freelance newspaper columnist, and TV anchor.

Samantha Ducloux Waltz ("Converting Ray") is a freelance writer in Portland, Oregon. Her work can be seen in a number of anthologies, including several volumes of the *Cup of Comfort®* series, and in *The Christian Science Monitor*. She has also published fiction and nonfiction under the name Samellyn Wood. She and her husband, Ray, share Annie, a golden retriever, and Naomi, a black kitty. Samantha's horse, Vida, lives nearby.

Dallas Woodburn ("Sweeter Than Ice Cream") has published two collections of short stories, and her work has appeared in several magazines, including *Family Circle, Writer's Digest, Cicada,* and *Writing*. She is the founder of Write On!, a nonprofit organization that encourages kids to read and write. She is working toward a creative writing degree at the University of Southern California.

Tell Your Story in the Next *Cup of Comfort*®

We hope you have enjoyed *A Cup of Comfort*® *for Dog Lovers* and that you will share it with all the special people in your life.

You won't want to miss our next heartwarming volumes, *A Cup of Comfort*® *for Single Mothers* and *A Cup of Comfort*® *for Horse Lovers*. Look for these new books in your favorite bookstores soon!

We're brewing up lots of other *Cup of Comfort*® books, each filled to the brim with true stories that touch the heart and soothe the soul. We would love to include your stories in upcoming editions of *A Cup of Comfort*®.

Do you have a powerful story about an experience that dramatically changed or enhanced your life? A compelling story that can stir our emotions, make us think, and bring us hope? An inspiring story that reveals lessons of humility within a vividly told tale? Tell us your story!

Each *Cup of Comfort*® contributor will receive a monetary fee, author credit, and a complimentary copy of the book. Just e-mail your submission of 1,000 to 2,000 words (one story per e-mail; no attachments, please) to:

cupofcomfort@adamsmedia.com

Or, if e-mail is unavailable to you, send it to:

A Cup of Comfort
Adams Media
57 Littlefield Street
Avon, MA 02322

You can submit as many stories as you'd like, for whichever volumes you'd like. Make sure to include your name, address, and other contact information and indicate for which volume you'd like your story to be considered. We also welcome your suggestions or stories for new *Cup of Comfort*® themes.

For submission guidelines please visit our Web site: *www.cupofcomfort.com*.

We look forward to sharing many more soothing *Cups of Comfort*® with you!

About the Editor

Colleen Sell has compiled eighteen volumes of the *Cup of Comfort*® book series. She has also authored, ghostwritten, or edited more than 100 books, published dozens of magazine articles, and served as editor-in-chief of two award-winning consumer magazines. Colleen and her husband, T.N. Trudeau, share a turn-of-the-century farmhouse on forty acres in the Pacific Northwest, which they are slowly turning into an organic lavender and blueberry farm. Their border collie/Austrian shepherd, Woodstock, watches over it all with amusement.

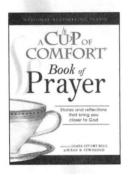

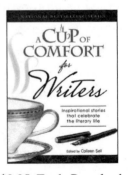